Show Me The Scripture

Because Jim Jones was A Helluva Preacher Too

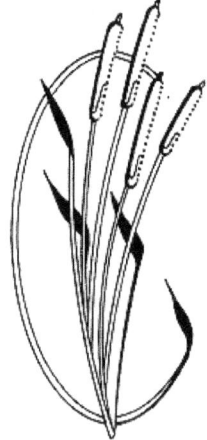

Show Me The Scripture

Because Jim Jones was A Helluva Preacher Too

by Brother James

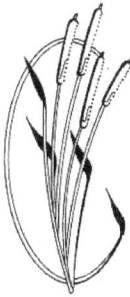

Editor
Ray Glandon

Original Cover Concept
Brother James

Cover Artwork
Tim James

Book Cover Photography
CC Photography Enterprises, L.L.C.

Book Cover Editing
Steven Hill

Senior Publisher
Steven Lawrence Hill Sr.

Awarded Publishing House
ASA Publishing Company

A Publisher Trademark Copy page

ASA Publishing Company
Nominated for the 2012 Better Business Bureau Torch Award
105 E. Front St., Suite 101, Monroe, Michigan 48161
www.asapublishingcompany.com

All Rights Reserved. No part of this publication may be reproduced, stored in a retrieval system or transmitted in any form or by any means electronic, mechanical, photocopying, recording or otherwise, without the prior written permission of the publisher. Author/writer rights to "Freedom of Speech" protected by and with the "1st Amendment" of the Constitution of the United States of America. This is a work of fiction. Any resemblance to actual events, locales, person living or deceased is entirely coincidental. Names, places, and characters are within the work of fiction and its entirety is from the imagination of its author.

Any and all vending sales and distribution not permitted without full book cover and this title page.

Copyrights©2014, Brother James, All Rights Reserved
Book: Show Me The Scripture *Because Jim Jones was A Helluva Preacher Too*
Date Published: TK
Edition 1 *Trade Paperback*
Book ASAPCID: 2380642
ISBN: 9781886528802
Library of Congress Cataloging-in-Publication Data

This book was published in the United States of America.
State of Michigan

A Publisher Trademark Title page

Table of Contents

Preface ix

Dedication xiii

Chapter 1   Spoon-fed Christians 1

Chapter 2   The Myth of Fasting 9

Chapter 3   Praising God: Must Be Uniform
in the Corporate Setting? 14

Chapter 4   Speaking in Tongues:
Myth versus Scriptural Reality 20

Chapter 5   Pastor's Authority: Is Your Pastor
a god on Earth? 34

Chapter 6   The Myth of the Prosperity Gospel 44

Chapter 7   Myth of Christian Tithing versus
the Truth of Christian Giving 58

Epilogue   In the Final Analysis 75

Preface

When you read this work you will come to the conclusion that I am a very opinionated individual. However, I want you to know that my opinions are generated from what I have read and absorbed in the teachings from the men and women of God whom I sincerely respect. These men and women of God are truly worthy of "Double Honor"!

In his notable work, *African Religions and Philosophy,* John S. Mbiti states, "African people are a notoriously religious people." As a PK, a Preacher's Kid, I find that statement has tremendous merit. However, what I feel is lacking in the African American Churches of today is a desire of its congregants to truly "study to show ourselves approved." What I see are churches with hundreds and even thousands of members with less than ten percent of their members attending the weekly Bible Study and/or Sunday School, if a Sunday School exists! Some pastors are so vain, they think they are the only ones capable of espousing and teaching the Word of God. Consequently, they do not allow Sunday School in any form or directed to any age group! I suspect these pastors feel intimidated by some of their well-read congregants with the Spiritual gift of teaching (some have the gift to teach). Sunday School or some type of Sunday Bible class has always been an integral part of the African American religious tradition.

Okay, let me get off my soap box as I do have a tendency to digress. What I see is a great need for a mindset as presented in the Book of Acts, chapter seventeen, verse eleven: where the New International Version (NIV) reads, *"Now the Berean Jews were of more noble character than those in Thessalonica, for they received the message with great eagerness and examined the Scriptures **every day** to see if what Paul said was true."* What I see as a Sunday School teacher and Bible Study facilitator with an insatiable appetite for the Word of God are people who are totally reliant on the Gospel as espoused by their pastor. They accept as truth everything their pastor says, without question. They trust and expect their pastor, as their shepherd, to provide them on every Sunday with a sumptuous spiritual feast. These same congregants leave their house of God full of something (I said earlier I am a PK, so I will not share with you what I know some of these folks are full of), and if they were asked three to five hours later what their pastor's sermon was about, their response would more than likely be, "I can't remember, but he/she sure did preach!" We sometimes get caught up in the hype of the music and whooping, or as Richard Pryor once said, "we get a show for our money!" These congregants look at their pastor as if he or she were a living God, not realizing that a shepherd was one of the lowest positions one could occupy in any ancient society, especially that of the ancient Israelites. These congregants act, think and are governed just like sheep, not realizing that some of their shepherds are leading them astray like lambs being led to slaughter. They choose to be "spoon-fed!" I have always said that too many African American churchgoers have the following routine: They have a special place where they keep their Bible, only to retrieve it from this special place on their way out the door as they head to Church. Upon arriving at their place of worship, they only open their Bible upon the instructions of their pastor or other worship leader, such as a deacon. After reading the selected text as instructed, they close their Bible and listen to the music and the sermon. When service is over and they return home, they place their Bible in its special place, never touching it until the next time they go to church or when they are dusting that particular area because company is coming.

The question that now arises is, is that mode of spiritual operation appropriate or inappropriate? I respectfully suggest that that is not what God expects of His children. He has blessed us with the gift of life and the chance of salvation, which leads to eternal life if only we accept Him. But NO, we would rather spend endless hours watching inane mind-numbing reality television shows, such as the "Biggest Loser" or the "Housewives" of someplace. If you ask me, and I know you will not, the biggest loser is the person who can find nothing better to do with his time. To paraphrase Karl Marx, the author of the Communist Manifesto, "reality television is the opiate, the pain killer of the masses of the people!" We might want to look to the heavens from whence cometh our help!

"Well, Brother James, that seems mighty haughty, pompous and even egotistical of you! You sound like one of those 'holier than thou' folks who would have everyone else believe they sit at home only listening to religious music, reading religious text and watching religious television shows!!" Well, my sisters and brothers, that is not true. I listen to all forms of music, even some Rap. I read all types of literature, history and novels, etc. and I love mystery and comedies on TV. However, at the same time, I realize that I must dedicate some time, some serious time to my own spiritual development and not leave it up to some pastor who just may have as many problems or issues as I do. Jesus was the only perfect being to ever exist, but we entrust our futures in eternity to some man or woman who has failings and issues just like us. As the son of a Baptist Pastor, I have seen men and women in the pulpits across this country that had substance abuse issues, cravings for money, status and power and an inability to control their lustful desires for someone of the opposite sex who was not their spouse and/or issues with their sexual identity. And, heaven forbid if these pastors were to discover that someone in their congregation was perceived as having more biblical knowledge than they possessed. That person or persons would have to go, as expeditiously as possible.

Many of us African American congregants also invest too much of our financial resources by being conspicuous consumers. The phrase, "dress to impress" had to be a direct result of our desire to be perceived as being more than what we really are in our communities as opposed to dressing appropriately for a job interview. We buy the biggest and most expensive cars, homes, plasma screen TV's, the best designer clothes and footwear, but we will not spend any serious money to buy biblical research tools such as a Study Bible, a Bible Dictionary, a Concordance, and or/a Bible Commentary. No, we would rather, as Pastor Jake Gaines, Pastor of Synagogue Baptist Church in Detroit, a true and serious man of God says, "spend a $1,000 on a Big Screen TV and buy a $3.99 Bible." Do we really think that is what God wants? Of course not.

"So, Brother James, why are you saying these somewhat harsh and condemning things? Have you set yourself up as the final arbitrator of all that is good and bad in the 'Houses of Worship' in the African American community?" Certainly not! All I am saying is that in these days when we see God obviously cleaning house by knocking some of the most popular and prominent men and women in ministry off their once pristine, above—reproach pedestals, we must STOP trusting our salvation to them and become like the Bereans of old. We must study the Word of God as if our very lives depend on it. Because in the final analysis, it does!

Dedication

I sincerely dedicate this book to the following men of God whose care and nurturing of their respective flocks provided me with a model for the "near" perfect preacher/teacher. Their pastoring was and is as close as anyone could get to that of our Lord and Savior Jesus Christ's who my late Father always said was the model for every preacher/pastor.

    Pastor Marshall B. Lanier (Deceased)—Lanier Baptist Church—Louisville, Kentucky

    Pastor Horace C. Mitchell (Deceased)—Hill Street Baptist Church—Louisville, Kentucky

    Pastor Valmon Stotts—Unity Baptist Church—Detroit, Michigan

    Pastor Joseph Chatten—Resurrection Mission Baptist Church—Berkley, Michigan

    Pastor Jake Gaines—Synagogue Baptist Church—Detroit, Michigan

    My late father, Pastor Robert Walter James, pastor of Pleasant Point Baptist Church—Utica, Kentucky

    Finally, I also dedicate this work of nonfiction to my late mother, Mrs. Juanita Mae Alexander James. She was the greatest Sunday School Teacher and personification of what it truly means to be a Christian who showed herself approved!

    Father God, I sincerely thank you for decreeing that I would emanate from the family that I did. My parents and others helped shape my spirituality and hunger for your Word. I pray that I will be spiritually reunited with them in Heaven.

Brother James

Show Me The Scripture

Because Jim Jones was A Helluva Preacher Too

by Brother James

Chapter 1

Spoon-fed Christians: How Some Preachers are Spiritually Poisoning their Naïve and Spoon-fed Congregations thereby Leading them to Spiritual Slaughter

[11]Now the Berean Jews were of more noble character than those in Thessalonica, for they received the message with great eagerness and examined the Scriptures **every day** to see if what Paul said was **true**. [12]As a result, many of them believed, as did also a number of prominent Greek women and many Greek men. **(Acts 17:11-12 NIV)**

If you are over forty, you probably remember hearing the news accounts regarding the "Jonestown Massacre" of November 18, 1978. James "Jim" Warren Jones, a charismatic preacher, community activist and quasi politician led over 900 of his members in a suicide pact in a communal compound in a very remote region of Guyana. Jones started his career as a religious leader in rural Indiana, then rose to become one of the most celebrated religious leaders of his day. He established a church in San Francisco known as the "People's Temple." The members of the Temple came from all walks of life (race, color, creed, socio-economic status, etc.) To his congregation, Jim Jones apparently appeared as a Jesus-like figure. It was widely reported that

Jim Jones fed the hungry, provided jobs and money to the poor and needy, provided health care to those who could ill-afford it, and housing to those who were homeless. Jim Jones seemed to always find a way through his persuasive, oratorical gift and charismatic powers, political and financial connections and influence to get whatever his congregants needed to sustain themselves. In many ways Jim Jones became his flock's Messiah!

It appears that Jones learned that his alleged cult was the object of a congressional inquiry led by, congressman Leo Ryan. The impetus for this congressional inquiry was information presented to the mass media and Congress by family and friends of those members of the People's Temple who thought Jim Jones was taking financial advantage of his mesmerized congregation. Some of these congregants had financial means while it was alleged that the poor members gave their social security and public assistance checks over to Reverend Jones.

These disgruntled friends and family members viewed Jim Jones as a charlatan, a pimp in the pulpit, a Judas goat who was leading his huge congregation to Satan's slaughterhouse, robbing them of any chance of going to heaven.

So, Brother James, why are you suggesting that Jim Jones, of The People's Temple, was a Judas Goat? He was just a misguided preacher, was he not? Not by a long shot! Let us look at the Wikipedia.com definition of a "Judas Goat"! "A Judas goat is a trained goat, used at a slaughterhouse and, in general, animal herding. The Judas goat is trained to associate with sheep or cattle, leading them to a specific destination. In stockyards, a Judas goat will lead sheep to slaughter while its own life is spared. Judas goats are also used to lead other animals to specific pens and onto trucks. The term is a reference to the biblical character, Judas Iscariot."

My sisters and brothers, there are a lot of Jim Joneses in the pulpits across this country today who are leading their congregations astray, to Satan's slaughterhouse. Please remember that a Judas goat led sheep and cattle to their deaths. If you are a Christian, then you are part of Jesus' flock of sheep and Jesus' voice is the only one that will lead you to heaven!

I respectfully suggest that these Judas goats in the pulpit are not much different than Jim Jones, who led over 900 people, including children, to perish in the jungle of Guyana by drinking a poison-laced Kool-Aid type of drink. You do not have to drink a Big Gulp cup of spiritually poisoned Kool Aid in the form of a sermon or other teachings all at once to lose your eternal life. No, you can be poisoned slowly with a potent, but in small doses, poison like arsenic. In the past, people used arsenic to slowly kill others for financial gain or to get out of a bad relationship of which they grew weary. Arsenic is a common poison that we are born with in our system. It is in small amounts in the air we breathe, the water we drink, and is present in the soil from which the fruits and vegetables we eat are grown. However, like most anything else, a little arsenic is not harmful, as we all have a threshold for arsenic and other forms of poison. But, if we are fed some extra doses of satanic arsenic from the pulpit for an extended period of time, we will surpass that poison threshold. So, I liken every time we hear a sermon that is not rooted in God's word to our being *slowly, spiritually* poisoned. When we are given a distorted version of God's Word, we are slowly being given doses of a satanic form of arsenic. It is a satanic form of arsenic that, after an extended period of time, will surpass our threshold of being spiritually poisoned and lead to our spiritual growth being stunted and possible spiritual death looming.

One day after enduring this methodically slow imbibing of satanic arsenic over an extended period, we will discover, when there is nearly irreparable damage, that we are potentially taking in our last spiritual breath. Our spiritual focus on the Lord will be replaced with some distortion of God's Word, and we will ignore God's law and adhere to the self-made laws of some false preachers or teacher. Again, we can take the one time Big Gulp Cup full of spiritual poison and spiritually die, or we can take in the spiritual poison of these false teaching pastors and spiritually die a little at a time. In the final analysis the end result is one and the same! **We will not lose our salvation if we are saved, but we will not have learned the true meaning of God's Word and be believers of false doctrine.**

How are we spiritually poisoned? Okay! When any pastor teaches us that "sowing a seed" for his or her ministry will get us to heaven without focusing on the Gospel of Jesus Christ. When any pastor suggests that our focus should be on acquiring material things as opposed to "seeking first the kingdom of heaven." When a pastor tells us he has the road map to heaven and that it includes a gospel of "name it and claim it." When the pervasive prosperity gospel is first and foremost or when a gospel that makes that pastor a god on earth! If these are the sermons you are hearing, then we are being led astray. We are being spiritually poisoned.

There is in my mind a major difference between a religion and a cult. Jim Jones, in the minds of many educated people, was a cult leader, not a religious leader. So let us make the distinction between a religion and a cult.

Wikipedia defines religion thusly: Religion is an organized collection of belief systems, cultural systems, and world views that relate humanity to spirituality and, sometimes, to moral values. Many religions have narratives, symbols, traditions and sacred histories that are intended to give meaning to life or to explain the origin of life or the Universe. From their ideas about the cosmos and human nature, they tend to derive morality, ethics, religious laws or a preferred lifestyle. According to some estimates, there are roughly 4,200 religions in the world.

Many religions may have organized behaviors, clergy, a definition of what constitutes adherence or membership, holy places, and scriptures. The practice of a religion may also include rituals, sermons, commemoration or veneration of a deity, gods or goddesses, sacrifices, festivals, feasts, trance, initiations, funerary services, matrimonial services, meditation, prayer, music, art, dance, public service or other aspects of human culture. Religions may also contain mythology.

The word *religion* is sometimes used interchangeably with *faith* or *belief system*; however, in the words of Émile Durkheim, "religion differs from private belief in that it is 'something eminently social'. A global 2012 poll reports that 59% of the world's population is religious, 23% are not religious, and 13% are atheists." We can assume at this point, based upon the Wikipedia data that 5% of the world's population have no idea as to their religious belief system.

What must be understood at this point is that Christianity is a religion based in the belief of Almighty God as part of the Godhead or Trinity (The Father, The Son and the Holy Spirit). As religious Christians we are to concern ourselves first with the gospel of Jesus Christ and his commandments, that we are to love God with all our hearts, and love others as we love ourselves. We must study to show ourselves approved so we might not fall sway to the teachings of any false doctrine that promotes a pastor as a deity on earth and/or the pursuit of material things.

Wikipedia states that the word cult in current popular usage usually 'refers to a new religious movement or other group whose beliefs or practices are considered abnormal or bizarre by the larger society The word originally denoted a system of ritual practices. The word was first used in the early 17th century, denoting homage paid to a divinity and borrowed via the French *culte* from Latin *cultus* "worship, from the adjective *cultus* 'inhabited, cultivated, worshipped,' derived from the verb *colere* "care, cultivate."'

Jim Jones was not a Christian pastor. He was an egotistical, megalomaniacal, perverted, cult leader, and there are some Jim Joneses today who, under the guise of Christianity, are nothing more than cult leaders. We must be wary of these pimps in the pulpit; these devils in sheep's clothing; these abusers of God's word for personal gain; these fake religious leaders.

The African American Church has a long history of preachers who were viewed as cult leaders who became rich as a direct result of their spoon-fed members. These spoon-fed members never did what the ancient Bereans did: check the scriptures daily to see if after hearing Paul and Silas teach, that it was in-line with God's word. This does not happen enough today as many spoon-fed Christians take what their religious leader, or should I say, cult leader has espoused from their respective pulpits as totally valid. Some of these cult leaders even had the audacity to tell their congregations they were gods on earth. Many were simply blessed with excellent speaking and researching skills which they used to enthrall their members.

In his renowned work, *Black Gods of the Metropolis: Negro Religious Cults in the Urban North,* Arthur Huff Fauset identifies the following African American churches from the past as cults.

- Mt. Sinai Holy Church of America, Inc.
- United House of Prayer For All People (Bishop ["Sweet Daddy"] Grace)
- Church of God (Black Jews)
- Moorish Science Temple Of America
- Father Divine Peace Mission Movement

It is a spiritual imperative that as Christians we do not fall under the spell of these greedy, self-serving, and evil so-called religious leaders whose only motive is to enrich themselves. God is showing us that we need to study more so we will not fall victim to false teachers who are substance abusers, some who even have been known to die from their substance abuse. Nor should we allow ourselves to be captivated by the eloquence of a man who has a penchant for prostitutes or whose sexual appetite is focused on unsuspecting and vulnerable young boys and girls. God does not want us to be enthralled by the articulate and homespun teachings of men and women whose folksy sermons lead us to believe that all we need do is "name it and claim it," because God will let us have whatever we want if only we have faith. If that were the case why was the Apostle John the only one of Jesus' disciples not to be martyred? Why wouldn't the prophets of the Old Testament or the martyred disciples "name it and claim it" that their teaching and preaching would be well received and applied by the people with whom they share God's will?

Finally, God does not want us to fall prey to preachers who have multiple mansions, private jets, limousines, and a bank account that could pay off a quarter of the national debt! Rather, God wants us to use our discernment and gifts of learning by reading our scriptures and using tools like a Bible Dictionary, a Concordance and a respected Commentary so we might show ourselves approved. God also expects us to have regular attendance, if possible, in some form of Bible Study, such as Sunday School.

Yes, it is imperative that we study and learn as much about the Lord as we possibly can because we can watch a 3 hour sports event, spend hours in a club, or watch a reality show that only promotes dysfunction, profanity and ways of living that are counter to God's word. We have a lot of time for nonsense but NO equivalent time for studying God's Word.

Please, show me the scripture where God says we are not to study His word and that we should entrust our salvation to hearing sermons that we do not research afterwards.

Please pray that God will guide you in your learning process because it is of tantamount importance in our goal of going to heaven. Our pastors cannot get us to heaven solely on the content of their sermons. They are like the GPS or MapQuest we use during our travels, but we must read the road signs along our spiritual path.

I am praying that you revert from being a lazy spoon-fed Christian, if that is the case, and become a self-fed Christian, one who studies commensurate to how God is blessing them!

Again, please, pretty please, show me the scripture that even remotely suggests we are to entrust our salvation to the preaching and teachings of our pastor ONLY!

Chapter 2

Show me the Scripture that Says God will Give You Whatever You Ask for if You FAST

[12]"Even now," declares the LORD, "return to me with all your heart, with fasting and weeping and mourning." **(Joel 2:12 NIV)**

A few years back, I was approached by a woman who knows that I teach Sunday School at the church I attend. She knew me from a few church related seminars I had conducted in the Detroit metropolitan area. The conversation went something like this, "Brother James, my pastor said that if I fast, God will give me all the desires of my heart, especially a Mrs. Degree (in essence a husband)! Is that true? Can you point me to the scripture or scriptures that will show me if I do fast, all my prayers will be answered?"

I responded, "Respectfully, I suggest that you talk to your pastor as I do not want to contradict what he is teaching you and others within his congregation." She was insistent, so I then said, "Okay, I do not believe that your fasting will be answered by God providing you with everything you desire. If it were that simple, wouldn't every Christian go on a fast to ensure their health, wealth and accumulation of all the material desires of their heart and any other areas in their lives where they felt a lacking?"

She responded, "Well, that makes sense, but would you do the research and let me know one way or the other if what my pastor said is correct?"

I did the research and found that fasting is NOT a Biblical requirement of God. In addition, no member of the Trinity remotely suggests that believers can be blessed with whatever they want in life if they fast for forty days. Fasting, I informed her, should be viewed more in the spiritual realm than the physical realm where one deprives himself of food and drink. Spiritual fasting was a means of purifying ourselves of fleshy or, should I say, carnal toxins and pollutants that would ultimately help us better communicate with God better. I suggested that instead of fasting physically: food, why not fast of something that gets in her way of spending more time in prayer, meditation, or reading and studying God's word. I asked, "why not stop watching your favorite Reality TV show that does absolutely nothing to help you have a closer relationship with God? Instead of reading that romance novel in one sitting, why not read an entire chapter of a book of the Bible each day for the forty day fasting period! Instead of spending endless hours a day getting caught up on the work or church or neighborhood gossip, why not use that same time to go to a quiet place in your residence and meditate on how good God has been to you? Fasting would also purge from our minds and physical systems impurities that possibly hinder our righteous communications with God."

Let us consult the Nelson's New Illustrated Bible Dictionary to gain some much needed insight into the Christian's role and rationale for fasting. Nelson's provides the following information related to fasting, "**Fast – Fasting**—going without food or drink voluntarily, generally for religious purposes. Fasting, however, could also be done for other reasons. It was sometimes done as a sign of distress, grief, or repentance. The Law of Moses specifically required fasting for only one occasion—The **Day** of Atonement. This custom resulted in calling this **day** "the **day** of fasting" (Jeremiah 36:6) or the Fast"(Acts 27:9).

Now I would never say that I am either an authority on English composition the most blessed analytical observer, but I do know that the word **DAY** is singular! So why would a pastor promote the notion that if one were to fast for 40 days, God would answer all his prayers? I have heard of the "name it and claim it" gospel; the "prosperity gospel," but I have never heard of the "Fast, and everything you desire will be given unto you gospel"! It seems any pastor and others who promote a similar doctrine on fasting need to study more because as it says in James 3:1, "Not many of you should become teachers, my fellow believers, because you know that we who teach will be judged more strictly." Judged more strictly! I assume that what James is saying is that those who teach and preach have a higher obligation to study so that they will not mislead their congregations by misinterpreting God's Word. That one verse should be the hallmark, the mantra of some of today's preachers and teachers because if they believe in heaven and hell, then they should ensure whatever doctrine they espouse is in line with the word of God.

Let us also consult the Wycliffe Bible Dictionary to gain some much needed insight into the Christian's role and rationale for fasting. "God never seems to command His people to fast regularly, unless the 'affliction of the soul' on the Day of Atonement."

On the question, "What Does The Bible Say About Fasting?" gotquestions.com shares,

Question: "Christian fasting—what does the Bible say?"

Answer: Scripture does not command Christians to fast. God does not require or demand it of Christians. At the same time, the Bible presents fasting as something that is good, profitable, and beneficial. The book of Acts records believers fasting before they made important decisions (Acts 13:2; 14:23). Fasting and prayer are often linked together (Luke 2:37; 5:33). Too often, the focus of fasting is on the lack of food. Instead, the purpose of fasting should be to take your eyes off the things of this world to focus completely on God. Fasting is a way to demonstrate to God and to ourselves that we are serious about our relationship with Him. Fasting helps us gain a new perspective and a renewed reliance upon God.

Although fasting in Scripture is almost always a fasting from food, there are other ways to fast. Anything given up temporarily in order to focus all our attention on God can be considered a fast (1 Corinthians 7:1-5). Fasting should be limited to a set time, especially when fasting from food. Extended periods of time without eating can be harmful to the body. Fasting is not intended to punish the flesh, but to redirect attention to God. Fasting should not be considered a "dieting method" either. The purpose of a biblical fast is not to lose weight, but rather to gain deeper fellowship with God. Anyone can fast, but some may not be able to fast from food (diabetics, for example). Everyone can temporarily give up something in order to draw closer to God.

By taking our eyes off the things of this world, we can more successfully turn our attention to Christ. Fasting is not a way to get God to do what we want. Fasting changes us, not God. Fasting is not a way to appear more spiritual than others. Fasting is to be done in a spirit of humility and a joyful attitude. Matthew 6:16-18 declares, "When you fast, do not look somber as the hypocrites do, for they disfigure their faces to show men they are fasting. I tell you the truth; they have received their reward in full. But when you fast, put oil on your head and wash your face, so that it will not be obvious to men that you are fasting, but only to your Father, who is unseen; and your Father, who sees what is done in secret, will reward you."

So we can see from this lengthy dissertation several things. One, fasting is not a Godly mandate. Two, fasting does not always have to involve our self-deprivation of food. Three, fasting is a purification process so we might gain a better spiritual line of communication with God. And four, neither God nor His Son, Jesus, promised that if we fast, all our desires will be met.

I reflect back to Old Testament that the primary reason for fasting was on the Day of Atonement, and atonement in the English language may be simply defined as reconciliation. The purpose of fasting then was for the people of Israel and us to reconcile ourselves with God to seek His forgiveness for those things we do and say that are not pleasing in His sight. Fasting, therefore, is a means to make amends for our sins.

Fasting will never lead to our becoming rich, better looking, more intelligent, more popular or any other such egocentric desire. Fasting, with proper motives, will only lead to our having a better level of spiritual communication with God.

So, if I am wrong, please show me the scripture that disproves what I have just postulated. God is ALWAYS in the blessing business, but He is **NOT** in the "if you fast, I will give you all the desires of our heart business."

CHAPTER 3

Show me the Scripture that Says We Have to Praise God in Unison and Loudly in the Corporate Setting

Praise the Lord
A Christian Perspective—Gospel.com
A Community of online Christian Ministries says:
"[Psalm 150] An exuberant psalm of praise to God—
praise for many reasons, and in many different ways."

There are some weak, insecure, inane and lacking self-esteem pastors whose sermons are so weak that they have to coerce their congregations through the fear of peer pressure to leap to their feet, shout, clap their hands, and provide their pastor with vociferous approbation! These insecure pastors are simply pandering for an amen that they feel they deserve but are not receiving! I know that the primary reason they are not getting the praise they feel they are due is because of their laziness. Too many preachers are relying too much on the Internet's Sermons on-line to find and plagiarize a sermon rather than relying on the Holy Spirit to give them a Gospel of Jesus Christ filled and blessed sermon. The last time I checked, there were approximately 15 million websites where one could easily copy another pastor's sermons, and some of these sermons date back to the American Colonial period. In addition, if one were to check for sermons on-line produced by African American/Black pastors, one would find approximately 3 million websites of sermons to be copied, plagiarized, etc.

You may even search by your denomination. I found one website that is apropos, germane to our present discussion entitled, "Hold on to Your Confidence and PUSH (PRAISE UNTIL SOMETHING HAPPENS)" by Ronnie McNeill. While Mr. McNeill's point is worthy, it is, in my mind, being misconstrued by these lazy pastors who want all the recognition that should be directed to God and not them!

The advent and availability of these websites take all of the work out of sermon preparation by a lazy pastor's failure to study to show him or herself approved! These lazy pastors use peer pressure statements such as, "if you truly love the Lord, you would be standing on your feet Right Now and giving the Lord some Praise!" Or, "Hasn't God been good to you? Then why aren't you on your feet shouting and clapping, giving Him the praise He is due?" The only praise being sought by these inane pastors is for themselves! They have not studied enough, nor have they placed their focus on God enough for their SHEEP to feel their message. In John 12:42-43, Jesus said on this subject, "[42]Yet at the same time many even among the leaders believed in him. But because of the Pharisees they would not confess their faith for fear they would be put out of the synagogue; [43]for they loved praise from men more than praise from God."

I believe these pastors believe in God but see themselves as gods. Please note, I used the lowercase [g]od for God, in my example. These pastors want their flocks to fear and revere them as if they were in fact gods, like the Old Testament Canaanite false god, Baal, whose priests the prophet Elijah confronted and almighty God demonstrated His uncontested and irrevocable power over.

The Apostle Paul also addressed this issue about religious leaders seeking the praise of men rather than the praise of God in Galatians 1:10, "[10]Am I now trying to win the approval of men, or of God? Or am I trying to please men? *If I were still trying to please men, I would not be a servant of Christ."* These pastors who seek the praise of their congregants rather than seeking the praise of God are doing themselves a major disservice. One day they will be held accountable for these actions and will be judged accordingly for seeking the praise of men.

I hope I do not sound as if I am hating on or harshly judging these fake pastors who are seeking praise for themselves, but I would like to think I am a reasonably intelligent Christian, one who truly knows the difference between bologna and steak. I had once asked the Sunday School class I teach, "If you never had a steak, is it possible someone could give you a thick slice of bologna, cooked well-done, garnished with sautéed onions and mushrooms, smothered with some steak sauce, served with a baked potato and some vegetable, and tell you it was a sirloin steak?" How would you know the difference? In order to know the difference, you must have seen both a steak and a piece of bologna, smelled a cooked piece of steak and a piece of bologna, and tasted a piece of steak and bologna to know the difference. I said all that to say that some pastors are giving their congregants bologna and convincing them they are eating steak. Too many congregants do not question their pastor's doctrine and, more importantly, the motives behind their sermons. Is there a life application coming forth from your pastor's sermon? Is your pastor's sermon designed to teach you the gospel of Jesus Christ as opposed to the false "name it and claim it" or the "prosperity gospels"? The Apostle Paul said it best in his epistle/letter to the church at Galatia that there is only ONE GOSPEL and that is the gospel of Jesus Christ, "I am astonished that you are so quickly deserting the one who called you to live in the grace of Christ and are turning to a different gospel— **which is really no gospel at all**. Evidently some people are throwing you into confusion and are trying to pervert the gospel of Christ. But even if we or an angel from heaven should preach a gospel other than the one we preached to you, let them be under God's curse! As we have already said, so now I say again: If anybody is preaching to you a gospel other than what you accepted, let them be under God's curse!" I, for one, am not one of Pavlov's dogs!

I respectfully suggest these pastors I have been alluding to are using the Pavlov's "CONDITIONED REFLEX" behavioral influences method which insults me to the infinite degree! You remember the invaluable research of Ivan Pavlov, the Russian physiologist and behavioral scientist who had some dogs in cages and fed them every time a bell would ring? After a while these dogs would instinctively salivate upon hearing the bell ring whether any food was dropped into their cages or not. Pavlov proved that animals and people could be trained or conditioned to react to a stimulus even when the reward for reacting to the stimulus was absent. That is what many weak pastors of today do when they try to coerce and use peer pressure to get a standing ovation from their congregations by simply using stimuli statements such as, "If God has blessed you this week, you should be on your feet giving Him some praise!" These pastors have their congregations conditioned to react and respond by admonishing them to give praise to God on demand! Wow! And too many people are so naïve that they fail to see they are reacting like the dogs Pavlov used to test his conditioned reflex theory. Now, do not get me wrong, or as it is said in the vernacular of the streets, don't get it twisted! I have absolutely no problem when a pastor tells his or her congregation that God is worthy of praise. My problem commences when they tell their congregation HOW AND WHEN TO PRAISE GOD!

So, where is the scripture that says the only way to praise God is by every member of a church during a worship service leaping to their feet, then, in a uniform fashion, join their fellow congregants by stomping their feet, clapping their hands, jumping for joy, and in a chorus-like manner shout something like, "Thank You, Jesus! Thank You, Jesus!"

Please show me the scripture that says I must, upon direction from a pastor, react in the midst of his or her sermon like I was one of Pavlov's dogs! I could be wrong about these pastors, but again, someone must show me the scripture showing Biblical examples where God demands such form of praise! I am not the most intelligent student of the Bible, but I know that there are multiple ways to praise God and that we do not all have to be uniform to be unified in our praise and worship of God. Anything other than this is not truly representative of what God has allowed us to know about Him through His prophets, devoted followers like Abraham, David, the Disciples, the Apostle Paul, and most importantly, His only begotten Son, Jesus!

Nelson's New illustrated Bible Dictionary states in part, "Our praise toward God is the means by which we express our joy to the Lord. We are to praise God both for whom He is and for what He does (Psalm 150:2) Praising God for who He is, is called adoration; praising Him for what He does is known as thanksgiving. Praise of God may be in song, or prayer. Individually or collectively, spontaneous or prearranged, originating from the emotions or from the will." The Holman's Illustrated Bible Dictionary further states in part on our theme of praise, "Praise is to originate in the heart and not become [a] mere outward show (Matthew 15:8)."

There are numerous Biblical warnings in both the Old and New Testament that tell us of fake preachers who seek the praise of men rather than the praise of God. There are also many warnings of fake preachers who will attempt to lead us astray. The preachers I have alluded to are very vainglorious and egocentric men and women who must be avoided at all cost. The warning in 2 Corinthians 11:13-15 is so profound at this juncture. "For such men are false apostles, deceitful workmen, disguising themselves as apostles of Christ. And no wonder, for even Satan disguises himself as an angel of light. So it is no surprise if his servants, also, disguise themselves as servants of righteousness. Their end will correspond to their deeds."

I am thoroughly convinced that 'I' may praise God in any way He approves and that even in the corporate setting I am NOT obligated to be uniform and to stand and clap and shout upon the direction of my pastor. I may simply sit in my seat and cry, murmur praise, or even meditate my praises to God while others are standing, shouting, clapping etc. Again, I am not going to be conditioned to praise God in a uniform manner unless that is my own emotional response to praising God.

Please show me the scripture where I am obligated to be a pastor's equivalent to one of Pavlov's dogs, in terms of uniform corporate praise. No one can show me any Biblical mandate in this regard.

CHAPTER 4

Show me the Scripture where an Entire Congregation is Blessed by Speaking in Tongues

Now, brothers and sisters, if I come to you and speak in tongues, what good will I be to you, unless I bring you some revelation or knowledge or prophecy or word of instruction? **(I Corinthians 14:6 NIV)**

Several years ago, I delivered a presentation entitled, "Blacks in the Bible" as part of a Black History Month program at work. Later that day a young African American female co-worker approached me and asked if I would be willing to make this same presentation at her church. I indicated that I was willing if the date she was interested in fit my schedule. She then said, "Well, if you speak at my church, you must be able to speak in tongues because everyone at my church speaks in tongues."

I then graciously declined her request for me to speak at her church by saying, "I am sorry. I have never spoken in tongues, and if there is a requirement that I MUST SPEAK in TONGUES, then I will not be able to make the commitment to speak at your church."

What I remember most about this conversation was not so much her requirement that I MUST speak in tongues but the expression on her face that led me to believe that she thought me to be a horrible, depraved, and detestable sinner because I said I had never spoken in tongues. Do I believe that people speak in tongues? Yes, but the Bible says that speaking in tongues is a spiritual "gift," and that not everyone in the body of Christ has that gift, but *some* people do. The following scripture from the New International Version (NIV) of God's word bears this point. I Corinthians 12:4-11, reads, "[4]There are different kinds of gifts, but the same Spirit distributes them. [5]There are different kinds of service, but the same Lord. [6]There are different kinds of working, but in all of them and in everyone it is the same God at work. [7]Now to each one the manifestation of the Spirit is given for the common good. [8]To one there is given through the Spirit a message of wisdom, to another a message of knowledge by means of the same Spirit, [9]to another faith by the same Spirit, to another gifts of healing by that one Spirit, [10]to another miraculous powers, to another prophecy, to another distinguishing between spirits, to another **speaking in different kinds of tongues,** and to still another the **interpretation of tongues** (this is a key point that we will revisit later in this discourse). [11]All these are the work of one and the same Spirit, and he distributes them to each one, just as he determines."

In addition to my former co-worker, I can honestly attest to the fact that I have witnessed many prominent Cable TV preachers and some preachers in person who, in the midst of their sermons, blurt out some non-decipherable utterance, that only confound their message to me. Were they speaking in some ancient language? Were they blessed by the Holy Spirit to use their gift to speak, albeit quickly in this ancient unrecognizable "tongue" to their congregants? Was I supposed to be a beneficiary of these utterances? Given the fact that I did not understand, am I therefore not spiritual, holy, righteous and religious enough to understand these rapid fire grunts and mumbled utterances? I am confused as to why Almighty God would have a message presented by one of His Spiritual Leaders and I did not get the message in its entirety! Was there anything in these utterances that I missed that I need to become stronger in my faith and good works?

Was there a blessing for me and mine in this utterance that I would now miss because I neither recognized nor was able to understand? I have questions galore whenever I hear a preacher make utterances that sound like the lyrics of a Sly and the Family Stone song, "boom shaka laakka, ana takka lakka." Someone please help me understand why most Christian churches with hearing-impaired congregants will have a sign language interpreter; or an ethnically diverse Christian church will have a Spanish, Chinese, or Russian interpreter, etc., but in the House of God where speaking in tongues is a matter of routine, we do not have an interpreter for those occasions when the pastor or a congregant speaks in tongues? The reality that there is no interpreter present on such occasions truly mystifies me!

Does God love me less than the utterer? Hmm, maybe it is just me who is feeling left out! We need to clearly understand what the true Biblical meaning of the word "tongues" is in both the Old and New Testament.

To delve into our understanding of what the true Biblical definition of tongues is, we need to first look at the story of the Tower of Babel. This story is located in Genesis 11:1-9 where the NIV translation reads, "Now the whole world had one **language** and a **common speech**. As people moved eastward, they found a plain in Shinar and settled there. They said to each other, "Come, let's make bricks and bake them thoroughly." They used brick instead of stone, and tar for mortar. Then they said, "Come, let us build ourselves a city, with a tower that reaches to the heavens, so that we may make a name for ourselves; otherwise we will be scattered over the face of the whole earth." But the LORD came down to see the city and the tower the people were building. The LORD said, "If as one people speaking the same **language** they have begun to do this, then nothing they plan to do will be impossible for them. Come, let us go down and **confuse their language so they will not understand**

each other." So the LORD scattered them from there over all the earth, and they stopped building the city. That is why it was called Babel—because there the LORD **confused the language of the whole world.** From there the LORD scattered them over the face of the whole earth.

The most repeated word in this block of scripture is *"language,"* and the significance of that word for our understanding is that a *tongue*, Biblically speaking, is nothing more than a *language*. Webster's Dictionary defines *language* as follows: "*a*: the words, their pronunciation, and the methods of combining them used and understood by a community." Webster's defines a tongue as follows, "a: a fleshy movable muscular process of the floor of the mouths of most vertebrates that bears sensory end organs and small glands and functions especially in taking and swallowing food and in humans as a speech organ."

Let us now look at some Biblical sources to determine how the word ***tongue specifically relates*** to *languages* in the Holy Scripture.

The Wycliffe Bible Dictionary states that the word tongues, "is also used as a synonym for **language** or **dialect**," and provides Old and New Testament examples (Deuteronomy 28:49; Acts 1:19). Let us look at these scriptures from the King James Version (KJV) of the Bible for clarity's sake. Deuteronomy 28:49 reads, "The LORD shall bring a nation against thee from far, from the end of the earth, as swift as the eagle flieth; a nation whose **tongue** thou shalt not understand." Now Acts 1:19 reads, "And it was known unto all the dwellers at Jerusalem; insomuch as that field is called in their proper **tongue**, Aceldama, that is to say, The field of blood." Both examples substantiate my point that in these instances a tongue is no more than a recognized language used by a community of people to communicate one with the other.

The Nelson's New Illustrated Bible Dictionary sheds even more light on the Biblical nature of the gift of speaking in tongues. First, in defining the Biblical relevance of Tongues, the authors state, **Tongues, Gift of**—"The Spirit given ability to speak in *languages* not known to the speaker or in an *ecstatic language* that could not be normally understood by the speaker or the hearers." So given this definition, may we assume that an example of the gift of speaking in tongues in the present day would mean: if neither the pastor nor his congregation knew French, but he or she delivered a sermon in French, that, the congregation understood, is this a sign of the gift of speaking in tongues? I think so. Again, we are talking about a language such as English, French, or in the Biblical era, the Egyptian, Chaldean, Assyrian or Greek, etc., languages. A *recognizable language* by the people of a particular geographic region. I do not know Spanish, but I do have the ability to know when I am in the midst of someone who is speaking Spanish! I live in the metropolitan Detroit area. It is widely publicized that the metropolitan Detroit area has the highest concentration of people of Middle Eastern descent. I do not speak any Middle Eastern languages, but again, understand that a Middle Eastern language is being spoken when I am in the midst of people from that part of the world when they are having a conversation in their native or should I say ethnic "tongue."

But what is an ecstatic language? The word ecstatic literally means, "a state of being beyond reason and self-control; a state of overwhelming emotion; *especially*: rapturous delight; TRANCE; *especially*: a mystic or prophetic trance." Is that what happens in the 15 or less seconds a preacher utters again something akin to, the lyrics of a Sly & the Family Stone song, "Sha la ma cuca"?

Before I go any further, I want it clearly understood that I am not making fun of anyone who speaks in tongues, or should I say, believes they speak in tongues, or that they believe they are communicating with God. Rather, I am saying it is a Spiritual gift that not all people have, and when someone is speaking in tongues, if no one understands what they are saying, the message is not for the masses of the hearers. In addition, just as the Galileans spoke at length to all the assembled people of various languages, it should also be that someone who speaks in tongues today should also speak at length during their sermon or when they are praising God. **I respectfully suggest, that any spontaneous utterance of an unrecognizable language/tongue of 15 seconds or less is suspect at best!** Why do we not hear a sermon of at least fifteen minutes in "tongues"? I think at this juncture you know my answer.

Therefore, I do assert that it is impossible for an entire congregation to speak in tongues! I also assert that if an entire congregation is speaking in tongues in unison, then how can anyone of them benefit from what is being said? That would be akin to each member of their choir singing a different song at the same time. Who benefits from such a discordant situation? Paul was very careful about this issue as we will discover shortly.

Let me introduce a very controversial issue in some churches as it relates to speaking in tongues. Many Pentecostal and Charismatic churches promote the doctrine that speaking in tongues is the ONLY physical proof that a person has received the Baptism of the Holy Spirit at conversion. In a March 6, 2000, issue of *Christianity Today*, J. Rodman Williams wrote an article entitled *Should We All Speak in Tongues?* In this article Mr. Williams wrote, "One of the most influential and controversial events in the twentieth-century American church was the emergence of the charismatic movement. With its emphasis on the gifts of the Spirit, the movement brought elements of Pentecostalism to non-Pentecostal churches. By the early 1960s, Catholics, mainline churches, and many non-Pentecostal evangelicals were experiencing the power of the Holy Spirit through prophecies, divine healings, speaking in tongues, and various physical phenomena. The movement generated much debate about the purpose of these gifts and experiences in the Christian life. Were they legitimate expressions of worship, or just frenzied spiritual emotionalism?

Today, evangelicals seem to have made peace with the charismatic movement, embracing many of its practices and agreeing to disagree on others. Indeed, it's not strange these days to find people lifting their hands in the most conservative of evangelical functions. Despite this evolution, many questions remain about the meaning of speaking in tongues.

The phenomenon of tongues (or glossolalia) is identified by many as the supernatural utterance of foreign human languages (Acts 2:4,6); others contend that it includes speaking an angelic language (1 Corinthians 13:1) or some other verbal expression requiring interpretation (1 Corinthians 14). For many years, speaking in tongues was seen as the distinguishing characteristic of the Pentecostal and charismatic traditions within the church. Some Pentecostal Christians, in particular, laid heavy emphasis on speaking in tongues as "initial evidence" of baptism in the Spirit."

I heartily disagree with this notion that in order to be saved one must speak in tongues at the moment they accepted Christ as their Lord and Savior and sometime shortly thereafter. I stand pat on this position as the writings of the Apostle Paul clearly say over and again that, "Some" have the Gift of speaking in tongues. I believe that there is some confusion with the book of Acts being doctrine. Acts is simply the history of the formation of the Christian church. There are many deeds, and may I say miracles mentioned in Acts that are solely for our understanding of God's supremacy, sovereignty and mercy shown to us. I politely say again, everything in Acts should not be used or construed as the basis of Christian doctrine. If that were true, then why are not all Christian churches handlers of snakes as is mentioned in Acts 28:3-5 where Paul handled a viper (Snake) while shipwrecked on Malta. This is yet another Pentecostal belief and I should mention a belief shared by a small number of Pentecostals who tie the handling of snakes found in Acts 28:1-5 to the Gospels of Mark 16:17-18, "And these signs shall follow them that believe; In my name shall they cast out devils; they shall speak with new tongues; **They shall take up serpents**; and **if they drink any deadly thing, it shall not hurt them**; they shall lay hands on the sick, and they shall recover."

Again, I am not making fun of others beliefs, but if the previously mentioned scriptures are the basis of the belief that one must speak in tongues to be baptized in the Holy Spirit, should there not be a parallel then where churches drink a deadly poison at each service with a 100% survival rate? Remember Jim Jones???

Nelson's New Illustrated Bible Dictionary further states on the issue of the gift of speaking in tongues, "The gift of tongues is to be exercised with restraint and in an orderly way. The regulations for its public use are simple and straightforward. People who speak in an unknown language are to pray that they may interpret (I Corinthians 14:13), or, someone else is to interpret what is said. Each is to speak in turn. If these criteria are not met, they are to remain silent (I Corinthians 14:27-28). The gift of speaking in tongues and their interpretation are to be Spirit-inspired. Paul also points out that tongues are a sign to unbelievers. If these guidelines are not observed, unbelievers who are present will conclude that the people of the church are out of their minds. The phenomenon of speaking in tongues in the New Testament is not some psychological arousal of human emotions that results in **strange sounds**. This is a genuine work of the Holy Spirit."

Let us look at the Book of Acts where the greatest manifestation of speaking in tongues occurred at Pentecost. At Pentecost many people began to speak in tongues, languages unknown to them, and in addition, people were able to understand these languages that were heretofore unfamiliar to them. The Life Application New Testament Commentary on Acts 2:4 states, "at this point in this wonderful scene, Luke recorded that everyone present was filled with the Holy Spirit and began speaking in other languages. The 'filling' that occurred on Pentecost is called a "baptizing" and a receiving."

On this same issue the Believers Commentary on the subject of speaking in tongues states, "The occurrence of tongues on the Day of Atonement should not be used to prove that tongues are the invariable accompaniment of the gift of the [Holy] Spirit. If that were the case, why is there no mention of tongues in connection with:

(1) the conversion of the 3,000 (Acts 2:4);
(2) the conversion of the 5,000 (Acts 4:4); and
(3) the reception of the Holy Spirit by the Samaritans (Acts 8:17)."

Let us revisit the Nelson's New Illustrated Bible Dictionary for further clarity on speaking in tongues. "On the Day of Pentecost, the followers of Christ were all filled with the Holy Spirit and began to speak with other tongues, as the Spirit gave them utterance (Acts 2:4). The people assembled in Jerusalem for the feast came from various Roman provinces representing a variety of languages. They were astonished to hear the Disciples speaking of God's works in their own languages. Some have suggested that the miracle was in the **hearing rather** than the **speaking**. This explanation, however, would transfer the miraculous from the believing Disciples to the multitude who may have not been believers." Now lets us look again at the book of Acts Chapter 2 verses 5 through 12 in both the King James (KJV) and then the New International

Versions (NIV). The KJV reads as follows: ⁵And there were dwelling at Jerusalem Jews, devout men, out of every nation under heaven. ⁶Now when this was noised abroad, the multitude came together, and were confounded, because that every man heard them speak in his own **language**. ⁷And they were all amazed and marveled, saying one to another, Behold, are not all these which speak Galileans? ⁸And how hear we every man **in our own tongue**, wherein we were born? ⁹Parthians, and Medes, and Elamites, and the dwellers in Mesopotamia, and in Judaea, and Cappadocia, in Pontus, and Asia, ¹⁰Phrygia, and Pamphylia, in Egypt, and in the parts of Libya about Cyrene, and strangers of Rome, Jews and proselytes, ¹¹Cretes and Arabians, we do hear them speak **in our tongues** the wonderful works of God. ¹²And they were all amazed, and were in doubt, saying one to another, What meaneth this?

The NIV reads thusly, ⁵Now there were staying in Jerusalem God-fearing Jews from every nation under heaven. ⁶When they heard this sound, a crowd came together in bewilderment, because each one heard their own **language** being spoken. ⁷Utterly amazed, they asked: "Aren't all these who are speaking **Galileans?** ⁸Then how is it that each of us hears them in our native **language?** ⁹Parthians, Medes and Elamites; residents of Mesopotamia, Judea and Cappadocia, Pontus and Asia, ¹⁰Phrygia and Pamphylia, Egypt and the parts of Libya near Cyrene; visitors from Rome ¹¹(both Jews and converts to Judaism); Cretans and Arabs—we hear them declaring the wonders of God **in our own tongues!**" ¹²Amazed and perplexed, they asked one another, "What does this mean?" There are two things that must be considered here.

First, both versions of God's Holy word previously mentioned above indicate that a tongue is synonymous with a decipherable and established "foreign" language. Again, my assertion is that a **tongue** has to be a recognizable language by those who speak it or those people from another land or culture who hear it.

Second, the amazement of the multitude of people or hearers from different nations is found in their wondering how these "**Galileans**" were able to communicate proficiently in their individual languages or tongues. Why? The Galileans were not known to be the brightest of the bright or the icons of intellectualism of the ancient world! The Wycliffe Bible Dictionary states, "Galileans had different customs and simpler religious practices than the Judeans, so that the term Galilean was a reproach used by the Pharisees. People outside of Galilee had a poor opinion of Galileans and believed therefore that a prophet [Jesus Christ] could not come from Galilee. Thus the term Galilean signified both [a] geographical and cultural type." The MacArthur Bible Commentary further states on the subject of the Galileans, being viewed as ignorant and uncouth people; "**Galileans**— inhabitants of the mostly rural area of northern Israel around the Sea of Galilee. Galilean Jews spoke with a distinct regional accent and were considered to be unsophisticated and uneducated by the southern Judean Jews. When Galileans were seen to be speaking so many different languages, the Judean Jews were astonished."

It is worthy to note that the languages of the Old Testament that were translated into the English of the King James Bible were ancient Hebrew and Aramaic, the dialect of the Galileans, the dialect of Jesus Christ. This fact was yet another reason the Pharisees decided to ridicule and deny Jesus' Messianic mission here on earth. They pondered how someone who emanated from a rural community that fostered uncouth, uneducated, and unsophisticated people claim to be a Prophet of God, let alone the Son of God. How could Jesus, a Galilean, be the long awaited Messiah?

The New Testament was translated into the English of King James from the ancient Greek. Before the rise and supremacy of the Roman Empire, the then known world spoke and wrote in ancient

Greek due to the widespread rule of Alexander the Great. Certainly the people of the ancient world clung onto their languages, but the predominant language was Greek until the fall of the Greek empire and the emergence of the Roman Empire.

On this issue it is worth our time and effort to consult the Holman Bible Dictionary. Under the insert, Greek Language, we find the following definition: "Greek was spoken broadly across the Roman Empire. Alexander the Great (336-323, B. C.) conquered the known world and stipulated the spread of Greek culture, including the Greek language. This Hellenization established many characteristics of the Western world. Early Greek independent city states established individual dialects of Greek (Attic, Ionic, Doric). As a result of the conquests of Alexander, however, these dialects mixed together into a common tongue [there is that word again!], a 'Hellenistic Greek,' that has come to be called "Koine." This was the common language understood almost anywhere. Historically this language stream flows into Byzantine Greek and then on into Modern Greek. Hellenistic Greek is a better term than Koine to describe the Greek of the first century. Hellenistic Greek represents a multilevel spectrum of Greek. The bottom level was Koine Greek; Koine was the Greek of the street, that is, colloquial daily speech. ...All of the New Testament was written in Greek. This itself is an indication of how thoroughly Hellenized was the world into which Jesus and his disciples preached."

On this same subject the Wycliffe Bible Dictionary states, "Hellenistic Greek consisted of a literary and non-literary form. ... while the non-literary or Koine Greek was the everyday language of the masses."

So, why is this important? Our knowledge of the ancient languages of the New Testament should help us understand that were we so inclined, we should be able to record and then trace the alleged words spoken in tongues during church service back to an ancient language that had its etymological roots in KOINE Greek.

Just as a reminder on the widespread use of Koine Greek in the New Testament era, we might want to consult Wikipedia.com where we find the following basic definition of Koine Greek, "Koine (Greek for 'common') is a term that came to designate that broad, common form of non-literary Greek used by *Greeks in common speech among themselves and with other ethnicities, and used by various ethnicities in their communication with other ethnicities.*"

To further illustrate this point we might want to consult The Life Application New Testament Commentary that states, "The believers could speak in these other languages because the Holy Spirit gave them this ability. This is the clear teaching of the New Testament—that the Holy Spirit sovereignly determines which gift(s) a believer will have (I Corinthians 12:7, 11). **Furthermore, these gifts are meant to be used to build up the body of Christ**. How can we build up the Body of Christ if no one understood what was uttered in tongues?"

What we have come to understand is this: the Jews in the diaspora coming to Jerusalem for Pentecost from all parts of the "Then Known World" were totally amazed that these Galileans, who were supposedly uncouth and uneducated, were able to articulately and eloquently converse in their own tongues or languages. What they failed to comprehend at that juncture was that, with the assistance of the Holy Spirit, the Galileans were able to communicate with the assembled masses in a variety of ancient languages from such faraway countries as Libya and Egypt, northeastern Turkey, present day Iran, Rome, the Greek island of Crete, Greece, and the Arabian nations of today. God had a plan, and exercised that plan educating such a diverse group of believers at Pentecost.

This being said, please remember that the gift of speaking in tongues was manifested at Pentecost in the New Testament era!

Therefore, those languages mentioned in Acts, Chapter 2 would have to be traceable to the tongues of the people mentioned in the Table of Nations in Genesis Chapter 10. I suggest to you that obviously the tongues we should hear spoken in those churches today, where speaking in tongues is either done as a matter of routine or is a requirement, must be rooted again etymologically in God's Word. Should not a pastor who demands his congregation to speak in tongues be able to deliver a twenty plus minute sermon in tongues as opposed to just shouting out an undecipherable utterance that no one understands? Leaders of the Roman Catholic Church during certain ceremonies at the Vatican still speak in Latin, an ancient language/tongue, do they not? When Pope Benedict XVI resigned recently, it was widely reported that in his resignation speech he "softly" spoke in Latin, an ancient tongue. Does not the Roman Catholic Church still celebrate the "Latin Mass"? Entomologically speaking, Latin is the basis for many of the western European or what has come to be known as the "Romantic" languages. Do not Billy Graham, T. D. Jakes and other preachers of international renown have an interpreter who interprets their message when they speak in a foreign country? For a person who speaks in tongues today to not be able to validate the ancient language they are speaking, again tied back to ancient Hebrew, Aramaic of the Old Testament era or Koine Greek, the widespread used language of the people of the New Testament era, they are, as it is said in the vernacular of the streets, "perpetrating a fraud"!

If speaking in tongues is supposed to be a widespread Christian doctrine and practice, and if speaking in tongues is a physical sign that one is baptized in the Holy Spirit, then why did Jesus and the Apostles not speak in tongues on a regular basis? I respectfully rest my case! But if I am wrong, please **show me the Scripture** that proves me wrong!

CHAPTER 5

Show me the Scripture on Pastors' Absolute Authority in God's House

²⁵Jesus called them together and said, "You know that the rulers of the Gentiles lord it over them, and their high officials exercise authority over them. ²⁶Not so with you. Instead, whoever wants to become great among you must be your servant, ²⁷and whoever wants to be first must be your slave—²⁸just as the Son of Man did not come to be served, but to serve, and to give his life as a ransom for many." **(Matthew 20:25-28 NIV)**

In the final scene of the 1938 motion picture, "The Adventures of Robin Hood," starring Errol Flynn, Prince John (played by Claude Rains) is about to be coronated as King of England, deposing his brother, King Richard. The Bishop, who is performing the coronation of Prince John, in a very stern and fearful voice because Robin Hood is poking a dagger in his back. asks, "By what authority do you claim the throne of England?" I use this movie scene to illustrate a point of how we live in an era where supposed men and women of God are trying to depose the undeniable authority of Almighty God by setting themselves up as Kings and Queens, usurping the authority of God. Yes, I am talking about these preachers whose only goal is to enrich themselves by using the pulpit to preach some materialistic oriented gospel as opposed to the Gospel of Jesus Christ.

I Timothy 3:1-7 says, "Here is a trustworthy saying: Whoever aspires to be an overseer desires a noble task. Now the overseer is to be above reproach, faithful to his wife, temperate, self-controlled, respectable, hospitable, able to teach, not given to drunkenness, not violent but gentle, not quarrelsome, not a lover of money. He must manage his own family well and see that his children obey him, and he must do so in a manner worthy of full respect. (If anyone does not know how to manage his own family, how can he take care of God's church?) He must not be a recent convert, or he may become conceited and fall under the same judgment as the devil. He must also have a good reputation with outsiders, so that he will not fall into disgrace and into the devil's trap."

The previously mentioned scripture in my mind is equivalent to what in the business world one might call a 'position description.' A Position Description for holding the job of a pastor, and from where I sit, this position description is not being adhered to by many men and women of the cloth.

So scripturally, where does it say that the pastor/bishop/elder/apostle or whatever name the leader of a church goes by, has undisputed authority? Where does it say that she or he has the God-given right to demand that everything in the church they shepherd should go the way they choose as opposed to adhering to the Word of God regarding the role of the leader of a flock? Where does it say that all matters of the church are to be determined exclusively by that particular churche's leader? Where does it say that the church leader is never to be questioned on any issue and every member must be subservient to this leader at all times? I respectfully submit to you that the congregants at many of today's churches give their leaders carte blanche, and that is leading to the spiritual, and financial decay of the Body of Christ in that church. There are a lot of vipers in the pulpits. There are a lot of gangster mentality leaders in the pulpit! There are a lot of egocentric, megalomaniacal, everything-is-about-me men and women in today's pulpits who are leading their flocks astray. There are some false preachers with an "it's me and mine, and to hell with everyone else" attitude in the pulpits. All one has to do is to look at the various recent church scandals that are growing in number across this land. I ask, like the Prophet Jeremiah did in Jeremiah chapter twelve, "Why O' Lord do you allow this to happen? Why do you allow Your people to be duped by these crooks?"

We have already discussed the qualifications of a pastor located in I Timothy chapter 3. I think it imperative that we look at Acts 20:28-31 so we might clearly understand the roles and responsibilities of our pastor. Acts 20:28-31 NIV states, "[28]Keep watch over yourselves and all the flock of which the Holy Spirit has made you overseers. Be shepherds of the church of God, which he bought with his own blood. [29]I know that after I leave, savage wolves will come in among you and will not spare the flock. [30]Even from your own number men will arise and distort the truth in order to draw away disciples after them. [31]So be on your guard! Remember that for three years I never stopped warning each of you night and day with tears."

There are five roles and responsibilities that I see as being clearly defined for church leaders in this text:

1. Pastors are to be leaders of his/her assigned church and must tend to the well-being of their congregation's spiritual development, just like an ancient shepherd tended to his flock.

2. Pastors are to ensure that their congregation is spiritually **developed** and **truthfully** fed the Word of God, especially the Gospel of Jesus Christ.
3. Pastors are to be the defenders of their assigned church, even at the risk of their life. They must be vigilant and always on guard against any attempted evil and divisive incursions by Satan's minions.
4. Pastors are to set a Christ-like example of conduct by all they do and say, not just in God's House but every minute of every day (admittedly this is a difficult standard of conduct to adhere to).
5. Pastors are to protect the Word of God ensuring neither they nor anyone else ever distorts His Divine Word for any nefarious reason. James 3:1-2 best illustrates this point in the NIV translation. This scripture reads, "Not many of you should become teachers, my fellow believers, because you know that we who teach will be judged more strictly. ^{2}We all stumble in many ways. Anyone who is never at fault in what they say is perfect, able to keep their whole body in check."

Looking further in Acts, Chapter 20 verses 32-35, we see some personal stipulations or, should I say, additional requirements for pastors if they are to be effective in doing the work of God, "^{32}Now I commit you to God and to the word of his grace, which can build you up and give you an inheritance among all those who are sanctified. ^{33}I have not coveted anyone's silver or gold or clothing. ^{34}You yourselves know that these hands of mine have supplied my own needs and the needs of my companions. ^{35}In everything I did, I showed you that by this kind of hard work we must help the weak, remembering the words the Lord Jesus himself said: 'It is more blessed to give than to receive.'"

These personal stipulations or additional requirements for pastors are:

1. Pastors are to acknowledge the fact that they are sanctified (set apart) and they are to govern themselves accordingly in all they say and all they do.
2. Pastor are not to be covetous of others, especially their peers or congregants whom they perceived to be more blessed materially by God.
3. Pastors should be prepared to make their own living if they are not suitably supported financially by their church
4. In the business of giving versus receiving, pastors should desire to always be on the giving end. This, I believe to be both on the spiritual and financial end. Pastors should be the icons, best examples of giving in their respective church.
5. Pastors MUST be called to preach by God and not by themselves, led by impure motives such as money.

So, Brother James, what do you see as the boundaries or parameters of a pastor? Well, I am so happy you asked me that question. God's Word provides for certain limits of a pastor in exercising his/her role as a leader of a flock.

A pastor should be the primary prayer leader in the church ([14]Is anyone among you sick? Let them call the elders of the church to pray over them and anoint them with oil in the name of the Lord. James 5:14 NIV).

A pastor should also be a trained Biblical Counselor to assist the flock in their times of emotional, financial and/or spiritual distress

(^{3}Praise be to the God and Father of our Lord Jesus Christ, the Father of compassion and the God of all comfort, ^{4}who comforts us in all our troubles, so that we can comfort those in any trouble with the comfort we ourselves receive from God. ^{5}For just as we share abundantly in the sufferings of Christ, so also our comfort abounds through Christ. ^{6}If we are distressed, it is for your comfort and salvation; if we are comforted, it is for your comfort, which produces in you patient endurance of the same sufferings we suffer. ^{7}And our hope for you is firm, because we know that just as you share in our sufferings, so also you share in our comfort. II Corinthians 1:3-7 NIV).

    A pastor should share the authority of leading the church with others and not act as if he has the absolute authority in God's House. This authority must be shared with the other ordained ministers in the church. Where is the scriptural reference for this position? Well, first we must understand that during the first century AD, Paul and the other apostles established churches throughout the world. In each church they trained men to be "Elders," or the leaders of those established churches. These elders were by definition ministers in the churches who taught the Word of God and ministered to the needs of their respective congregations. The Nelson's New Illustrated Bible Dictionary states, "Elders were associated with James in Jerusalem in the local church's government (Acts 11:30; 21:18), and with the Apostles in the decisions of the early church councils (Acts 15). Elders were also appointed in the churches established during Paul's first missionary journey (Acts 14:23). Paul addressed the elders at Ephesus (Acts 20:17-35). Elders played an important role in the church life through their ministry to the sick (James 5:14, 15). They were apparently the teachers also in a local congregation. Additional duties [of an Elder] consisted of explaining the Scriptures and teaching doctrine (I Timothy 5:17; I Peter 5:5)." The Holman's Illustrated Bible collaborates and substantiates my position on this issue as it states in a section referencing elders in the New Testament era, "In the address to the Ephesian elders, Paul referred to them as overseeing the church and serving as *shepherds* of the church (Acts 20:28).... The qualifications in Titus 1:6-9 and I Timothy 3:1-7 apparently apply to elders. It becomes apparent that the elders were the spiritual leaders of the church."

The question as to whether or not a pastor should also share the authority of leading the church with the deacons whose position was established by the word of God (Acts 6:2-4) is up for debate! But again the question as to whether a pastor has absolute authority in his congregation is muted by the fact that God's word shows us that the elders of the first century church were equivalent to our present day associate and assistant pastors. Certainly the pastor of the church has the greatest responsibility to lead the flock, but I suggest that he or she should deliberate with the other ministers in all matters affecting that given body of Christ. (To the elders among you, I appeal as a fellow elder and a witness of Christ's sufferings who also will share in the glory to be revealed: ²Be shepherds of God's flock that is under your care, watching over them—not because you must, but because you are willing, as God wants you to be; not pursuing dishonest gain, but eager to serve; ³not lording it over those entrusted to you, but being examples to the flock. I Peter 5:1-3 NIV).

Pastors should also be able to resolve and avoid any doctrinal issues within their given body of Christ. There are many doctrinal issues based upon one's interpretation of God's Word. Pastors have the responsibility to study and pray that they present the Word of God using a hermeneutical approach as opposed to an **eisegetical** approach (an approach where the pastor puts more into scriptural interpretation than what God actually intended). An occurrence of where doctrinal clarity was sought occurred when the apostles and their disciples conducted the Council at Jerusalem in Acts 15 where the question was raised by the Hebraic Jewish Christian converts as to whether the Gentiles had to honor both the teachings of Jesus and the Mosaic laws.

A pastor should never show favoritism to any members of the flock because the end result will be strife and disunity in the body of Christ. God does not show favoritism (^{8}But for those who are self-seeking and who reject the truth and follow evil, there will be wrath and anger. ^{9}There will be trouble and distress for every human being who does evil: first for the Jew, then for the Gentile; ^{10}but glory, honor and peace for everyone who does good: first for the Jew, then for the Gentile. ^{11}For God does not show favoritism.

Hebrews 13:17 clearly defines our role as congregants in the Body of Christ. Nowhere is it implied in this scripture or any others that we are to be totally subservient to the capricious and arbitrary whims of our shepherd. Rather, the strongest implication is that we are to be in concert with their works, as they minister to us not making their Godly assigned task difficult, "Have confidence in your leaders and submit to their authority, because they keep watch over you as those who must give an account. Do this so that their work will be a joy, not a burden, for that would be of no benefit to you."

Please show me the scripture where a pastor has the unabridged authority or right to demean and subject members of his congregation to his/her humiliating ranting and ravings to the point of inflicting unbearable stress, censorship and emotional pain on said congregant. Please show me the scripture where the pastor has the God given authority to disobey the word of God on such issues as adultery, substance abuse, pedophilia, homosexuality and/or failure to pay their rightful share of taxes. In Matthew 22:21 Jesus said, "render unto Caesar what is Caesar's and unto God what is God's."

So many pastors are being caught in scandals alluded to above, and recently so many pastors and their wives who are co-pastors are being sentenced to extensive stays in federal penitentiaries for tax evasion, which is a felony. These pastors are not claiming all their compensation, especially where they have coerced the church's money manager to look the other way when that given pastor grabs a handful of cash from the collected offering. Some pastors have been caught in Ponzi schemes, bilking their own and other congregations out of their life savings due to their perceived godliness and authority in the Lord's House. And please show me the scripture where a pastor has the God given authority to be revered as if he were a god here on earth. Too many pastors demand this type of reverence from their flocks, and if a congregant does not go along with their pastor's mandate level of reverence and subservience, then they are ostracized and criticized from the pulpit to the point they are treated as a pariah by their fellow congregants in their church.

No, my point is there is absolutely no scripture that suggests that a pastor has supreme authority in God's House. A pastor should be a model of Christian excellence. A pastor should know the depth and breadth of their God given authority and govern themselves accordingly. Pastors' authority should be modeled after the words of the Apostle Paul in his first epistle/letter to the church in Thessalonica where he wrote, "^{3}For the appeal we make does not spring from error or impure motives, nor are we trying to trick you. ^{4}On the contrary, we speak as those **approved by God to be entrusted with the gospel**. We are not trying to please people but God, who tests our hearts. ^{5}You know we never used flattery, nor did we put on a mask to cover up greed—God is our witness. ^{6}We were not looking for praise from people, not from you or anyone else, even though as apostles of Christ we could have asserted our **authority**. ^{7}Instead, we were like young children among you, Just as a nursing mother cares for her children" **(I Thessalonians 2:3-7)**

So if I am mistaken about a pastor's authority, ***please show me the scripture*** so I might change my thinking and govern myself accordingly.

Chapter 6

Show me the Scripture that Accurately Promotes the "Prosperity" and "Name it and Claim it" Gospels

⁶But godliness with contentment is great gain. ⁷For we brought nothing into the world, and we can take nothing out of it. ⁸But if we have food and clothing, we will be **content** with that. ⁹Those who want to get **rich** fall into temptation and a trap and into many foolish and harmful desires that plunge people into ruin and destruction. ¹⁰For the love of money is a root of all kinds of evil. Some people, eager for money, have wandered from the faith and pierced themselves with many griefs. ¹¹But you, man of God, flee from all this, and pursue righteousness, godliness, faith, love, endurance and gentleness. **(I Timothy 6:6-11 NIV)**

There is a constant, an incessant refrain heard by many Christians in the African American Community and that refrain is, "I am getting tired of them begging for more money at my church!" However, there are a large number of Christians flocking to churches or supporting televised ministries that promote what has become known as the "Prosperity Gospel."

So what are the tenets of this new phenomenon of the "Prosperity Gospel"? The Brother James definition, simply put, is when a preacher espouses that the more money you put in the collection plate the more God will bless you. The prosperity gospel preachers use a new catch phrase as they exhort and, in my mind, extort money from their congregations. This new catch phrase is "plant a seed." It seems to me this doctrine promotes the idea that we can bribe God (who owns all things) with money! What a laughable concept. But all we need do is explore the various Christian Television networks and one will see a multitude of pastors of various denominations shouting to their congregations that they must "PLANT A SEED," where a seed is money, and in some instances it's money that the giver can ill-afford to give beyond their tithes and offerings, in order for God to bless them. How ludicrous! How heretical a posture to be espoused from any pulpit.

I have always held the position that before I criticize something or someone I must at the very least try to know as much about that thing or person as possible. For example, I do not like caviar, why? Not because I realize it is fish eggs but because I have tasted it! I found caviar to be slimy, salty and lacking any appealing presentation. So, I have the right to my opinion of caviar being "nasty" based on my exposure to it. With this posture in mind let us look at some respected reviews of the Prosperity Gospel.

Wikipedia, the Free on-line Encyclopedia, provides us with the following definition and brief history of the Prosperity Gospel. While this definition and brief history of the prosperity gospel is lengthy, it provides us with an excellent foundation for understanding this distortion of God's word via the "prosperity" and "name it and claim it" gospels by greedy preachers across this land!

"**Prosperity theology** (sometimes referred to as the **prosperity gospel** or the **health and wealth gospel**) is a Christian religious doctrine that financial blessing is the will of God for Christians, and that faith, **positive speech** [name it and claim it doctrine], **and donations** to Christian ministries will always increase one's material wealth. Based on non-traditional interpretations of the Bible, often with emphasis on the Book of Malachi, the doctrine views the Bible as a contract between God and humans: if humans have faith in God, he will deliver his promises of security and prosperity. Confessing these promises to be true is perceived as an act of faith, which God will honor."

Hold on, wait a minute! Let me stop right here and address a major misconception of the prosperity gospel. The Book of Malachi mentioned above was the last book of the Old Testament. My studies of God's Word have shown me that there was a 400 year period between the writing of the book of Malachi and the New Testament. This 400 year period is sometimes referred to as the Intertestamental period; the 400 Years of Silence; or the 400 Years of Darkness. The reason for the last two naming conventions is due to the fact that God had grown so weary of the disobedience of the ancient Israelites, especially the Levites before the coming of the Messiah, that he did not send them a prophet for 400 years. The Levites were entrusted with managing the tithes they collected from the other eleven tribes of Israel. The Levites were absolved from many societal and sustenance tasks such as the agrarian tasks of farming and sheep herding, and military service so they might dedicate all their time and efforts to maintain the Temple/Tabernacle. During the time of Malachi the ancient Israelites became frustrated with God, feeling He had deserted them, and they began to disobey His laws. The New International Version Study Bible relates to us this disobedience in the introduction to the Book of Malachi, "Doubting God's covenant love (Malachi 1:2) and no longer trusting His justice (Malachi 2:17; 3:14-15) the Jews of the restored community began to lose hope. So their worship degenerated into a listless perpetuation of mere forms, and they no longer took the laws seriously."

I shared this information just so we might understand that the often quoted scripture found in Malachi 3:8-10: ([8]"Will a man rob

God? Yet you have robbed Me! But you say, 'In what way have we robbed You?' In tithes and offerings. ⁹You are cursed with a curse, For you have robbed Me, Even this whole nation. ¹⁰**Bring all the tithes into the storehouse**, That there may be food in My house, And try Me now in this," Says the LORD of hosts, "If I will not open for you the windows of heaven And pour out for you such blessing That there will not be room enough to receive it.") was an admonishment to the Jews and especially the Levites during the time of Malachi because the Jews were negligent in their tithes, and, since the Levites inheritance was part of the collected tithes, they too were negligent in their obligation to God. Using the principles of hermeneutics we would understand that this admonishment to the Jews and Levites of Malachi's day is NOT applicable today!

The Baker Theological Dictionary of the Bible states, "Tithes were awarded to the Levites for their priestly service because they would not receive land in Canaan (Numbers 18:19-21). They too gave a tenth of what they received (Numbers 18:26)." So what we see in Malachi is that the Jews and the Levites neglected giving God their proper tithes because again, they thought God had deserted them by not making them a prosperous and powerful nation. The Jews not only held back a portion of their tithes to God but also the tithes to be given to the Levites. The Levites in turn upon receiving a decrease of their tithes did the exact same thing and gave less than their obligated tithes from the tithes provided them to maintain the Temple/Tabernacle.

We have seen this situation in the current depressed economy where many churches with large congregations have to go from multiple services back to one traditional service. People have stopped going to church regularly because they do not have the money to meet their financial obligations (mortgage, car payment, utilities, etc.) and tithe.

We are witnessing the fact that many churches are having a difficult time meeting their mortgages, and some have asked their pastors to take a pay cut. I am aware of a few pastors in Detroit who took it upon themselves to not accept a salary and just live off their retirement annuity. These are truly Godly men!

Going back to Malachi 3:8-10, the prosperity gospel preachers use this well-known scripture to coerce their congregants into giving while again this scripture was only intended to be a message to the Jews of Malachi's day as attested by the Wycliffe Bible Commentary on these verses (Malachi 3:8-10), "Apparently the Israelites had made a pretense of conforming to the law, presenting some tithes before God but not all those that the law required." The Believers Bible Commentary states on these same verses, "The New Testament teaches believers to give systematically, liberally, cheerfully, and as the Lord has prospered them, that is, proportionally. But no mention is made of tithing. Rather, the **suggestion is that if a** Jew living under the law gave a tenth, how much more should a Christian living under grace give. The reward for faithful tithing in the Old Testament was material wealth; the reward for faithful stewardship in the present age is spiritual riches."

Please remember that Malachi is in the Old Testament as we move forward in our discussion.

Another well-known and over used Old Testament scripture promoted by the prosperity gospel preachers is the Prayer of Jabez. Jabez, whose name in ancient Hebrew means, "He makes sorrow or height" was a man who simply asked God for a blessing. He is mentioned in I Chronicles 4:9-10 ("[9]Jabez was more honorable than his brothers. His mother had named him Jabez, saying, "I gave birth to him in pain." [10]Jabez cried out to the God of Israel, "**Oh, that you would bless me and enlarge my territory! Let your hand be with me, and** keep me from harm so that I will be free from pain." **And God granted his request."**). Now here is a man who is only mentioned once in two verses of one chapter in the Bible, but his prayer has gained so much currency that numerous books with the theme of asking God for what you want and planting a seed will make you prosperous have been published as if they were a Biblical Self Help Book to ensure prosperity. Many readers of the various Prayer of Jabez books have yet to capture the true meaning of this one man's, Jabez's prayer. The Believer's Commentary, on I Chronicles 4:9-10 states, "Here was a man who had a large concept of God and honored Him by seeking His blessing. Jabez was a man of faith, and the Lord took notice of it. But without faith it is impossible to please Him, for he who comes to God must believe that He is, and that He is a rewarder of those who diligently seek Him. (Hebrews 11:6 NIV "And without faith it is impossible to please God, because anyone who comes to him must believe that he exists and that he rewards those who earnestly seek him.") The question now arises, are those congregants who adhere to the tenets of the prosperity seeking God or Wealth? Are those adherents to the prosperity gospel faithful to God in all they do and say, or are they simply thinking about themselves when Jesus gave us the two commandments: love God with all our hearts and to love others as we love ourselves? Where are these commandments located in the doctrine of the prosperity gospel?

With that in mind let us continue with our definition of the prosperity gospel gleaned from Wikipedia.

"Proponents [of the prosperity gospel] teach that the doctrine is an aspect of the path to Christian dominion over society, arguing that God's promise of dominion to Israel applies to Christians today. The doctrine emphasizes the importance of personal empowerment, proposing that it is God's will for his people to be happy. The atonement (reconciliation with God) is interpreted to include the alleviation of sickness and poverty, which are viewed as curses to be broken by faith. This is believed to be achieved through visualization and positive confession and is often taught in mechanical and contractual terms.

It was during the Healing Revivals of the 1950s that prosperity theology first came to prominence in the United States, although commentators have linked the origins of its theology to the New Thought movement. The prosperity teaching later figured prominently in the Word of Faith **movement** and 1980s televangelism. In the 1990s and 2000s, it was adopted by influential leaders in the Charismatic Movement and promoted by Christian missionaries throughout the world, sometimes leading to the establishment of mega-churches. Prominent leaders in the development of prosperity theology include E. W. Kenyon, Oral Roberts, A. A. Allen, Robert Tilton, T. L. Osborn, and Kenneth Hagin.

Churches in which the prosperity gospel is taught are often non-denominational and usually directed by a sole pastor or leader, although some have developed multi-church networks that bear similarities to denominations. Such churches typically set aside extended time to teach about giving and request donations from the congregation, encouraging positive speech and faith. Prosperity churches often teach about financial responsibility, though some journalists and academics have criticized their advice in this area as misleading. Prosperity theology has been criticized by leaders in the Pentecostal and Charismatic movements as well as other Christian denominations. These leaders maintain that it is irresponsible, promotes idolatry, and is contrary to scripture. Some critics have proposed that prosperity theology cultivates authoritarian organizations, with the leaders controlling the lives of the adherents."

I pray that this lengthy definition and history of the prosperity gospel were helpful. So instead of preaching and teaching the Gospel of Jesus Christ, many pastors are teaching: if you give more money to God, He will bless you materially? I do not know, but it sure seems like the ones who are truly being blessed financially and materialistically are those men and women in the pulpit who live extravagantly while many in their congregations struggle from one paycheck to the next.

In 2007, some of these prosperity preachers caught the ire of Senator Charles "Chuck" Grassley (R-IA) who initiated a Senate probe into the financial affairs of six prominent prosperity gospel preachers. All of the prosperity gospel preachers investigated operated a mega church. Grassley and his committee investigated the financial affairs of: Kenneth and Gloria Copeland, Creflo and Taffi Dollar, Benny Hinn, Eddie L. Long, Joyce Meyer, and David Meyer and Randy White and ex-wife Paula White.

According to Wikipedia, "The probe investigated reports of lavish lifestyles by televangelists including: fleets of Rolls Royce's, palatial mansions, private jets and other expensive items purportedly paid for by television viewers who donate due to the ministries' encouragement of offerings." So I respectfully ask, who is prospering from the prosperity gospel, the congregants or their "prosperity" and "name it and claim it" gospel preaching pastors?

I firmly believe that if the pastor, elder, bishop or whatever title a supposed man or woman of a House of God goes by, drives an expensive car, lives in a mansion in the most preferred and elite suburb of his city but could easily find folks who live in abject poverty or people who in large numbers suffer from high crime rates, substance abuse and teenage pregnancy within a five mile radius of that given House of God, something is very, very wrong.

Some smart aleck might say after reading this, "Well my church is outside that five mile radius and in one of my communities' best neighborhoods so your position does not apply!" To that person I would say, "Well if your church is so far from the people who Jesus would want us to serve, the poor in spirit and money, the uneducated and undereducated, the destitute, sick and shut-ins, then there is something seriously wrong with both the location of your church and its role in your community." Where did Jesus spend most of his time and who did He spend most of His time with during His three year ministry? Not the wealthy, not the kings and aristocracy but with the forlorn, the poverty stricken, the blind, the lame, the deaf, mute and dumb. Do not take my word for it; read the synoptic gospels (Matthew, Mark and Luke) and my point will be confirmed. Who is getting financially blessed again?

Let us take another view of the Prosperity Gospel and its deceptive methodology. The following article is well worth our time as it exposes many negatives of the prosperity gospel and its proponents.

In her well written and notable article entitled, **The Prosperity Gospel**, published by The Washington Post on December 20, 2009, Cathleen Falsani, the religion columnist for the Chicago Sun-Times wrote, 'In the Gospel of Saint Matthew, we are told that Jesus said, "You cannot serve both God and money" and, "It is easier for a camel to go through the eye of a needle than for a rich man to enter the kingdom of God."'

The "prosperity gospel," an **insipid heresy**, whose popularity among American Christians has boomed in recent years, teaches that God blesses those God favors most with material wealth.

The ministries of three televangelists commonly viewed as founders of the prosperity gospel movement—Kenneth Hagin, Kenneth Copeland and Frederick K.C. Price—took hold in the 1970s and 1980s. One of the oldest and best-known proponents of prosperity theology, Oral Roberts—the television faith-healer who in 1987 told his flock that God would call him home if he didn't raise $8 million in a matter of weeks—died at 91 last week (December 15, 2009).

But the past decade has seen this pernicious doctrine proliferate in more mainstream circles. Joel Osteen, the 46-year-old head of Lakewood Church in Houston, has a TV ministry that reaches more than 7 million viewers, and his 2004 book *Your Best Life Now: 7 Steps to Living at Your Full Potential*, has sold millions of copies. "God wants us to prosper financially, to have plenty of money, to fulfill the destiny He has laid out for us," Osteen wrote in a 2005 letter to his flock.

As crass as that may sound, Osteen's version of the prosperity gospel is more gentle (and decidedly less sweaty) than those preached by such co-religionists as Benny Hinn, T.D. Jakes and the appropriately named Creflo Dollar.

Few theological ideas ring more dissonant with the harmony of orthodox Christianity than a focus on storing up treasures on Earth as a primary goal of faithful living. The gospel of prosperity turns Christianity into a vapid bless-me club, with a doctrine that amounts to little more than spiritual magical thinking: If you pray the right way, God will make you rich.

But if you're not rich, then what? Are the poor cursed by God because of their unfaithfulness? And if God were so concerned about 401(k)s and Mercedes, why would God's son have been born into poverty?

Nowhere has the prosperity gospel flourished more than among the poor and the working class. Told that wealth is a sign of God's grace and favor, followers strive for trappings of luxury they can little afford in an effort to prove that they are blessed spiritually. Some critics have gone so far as to place part of the blame for the past decade's spending binge and foreclosure crisis at the foot of the prosperity gospel's altar.

Jesus was born poor, and he died poor. During his earthly tenure, he spoke time and again about the importance of spiritual wealth and health. When he talked about material wealth, it was usually part of a "cautionary tale."

Wow! No one could have stated the case against the prosperity gospel any better. Ms. Falsani clearly shows us how these pimps in the pulpit are grossly misrepresenting the word of God for their own personal gain. How can they reconcile the position they push from the pulpit with the teachings of Jesus whose parable of **the young rich man** in Matthew 19:16-22 contradicts that the more you give the more you will have theory? My interpretation of the conversation between Jesus and the rich young ruler goes something like this. "Hey Jesus, what must I do to go to heaven?"? The rich young ruler asks. Jesus responded by saying, "Go sell **EVERYTHING** you own, give the proceeds to the poor then follow me"! The young rich ruler then said under his breath, "Are you crazy!" He went on to say, "Naw Jesus. You don't understand. How much is it going to cost me to go to heaven"? Jesus just stared at the rich young ruler who got Jesus' message and he simply walked away saddened because he had lots of loot and material stuff (again, I am using literary license here). Who was it that said, "Seek ye first the kingdom of heaven"? Oh yes, it was Jesus!

But there is another side of the prosperity gospel that we might want to consider, especially its impact. I suggest to you that the prosperity gospel is yet another "con game." Yes, I said it. The "prosperity gospel" and the "name it and claim it" gospels are con games. It is a long con like those long cons featured in such movies as *The House of Games* starring Lindsay Crouse and Joe Mantegna, *The Grifters*, starring Annette Bening, Angelica Huston and John Cusack, and the most popular con game movie of all time *"The Sting"* starring Paul Newman and Robert Redford.

In all these movies people were duped out of their meager to extensive finances due to their own greed and desire to prosper without putting in the necessary work. **There is an old adage, "if it looks too good to be true, it probably is!"** I love the definition of a con (confidence scheme) found in my beloved *Wikipedia.com*. "A confidence trick (synonyms include confidence scheme and scam) is an attempt to defraud a person or group after first gaining their confidence. A confidence artist (or con artist) is an individual, operating alone or in concert with others, who exploits characteristics of the human psyche such as dishonesty, honesty, vanity, compassion, credulity, irresponsibility, naïveté, or greed."

"The perpetrator of a confidence trick (or "con-trick") is often referred to as a confidence (or "con") man, woman or artist, or a "grifter.""

I respectfully suggest to you that the prosperity gospel is a long con because people, or should I say congregants and misguided believers are so enamored with their pastor that they fail to see the difference in how their pastor is living compared to their lifestyle. They see their pastor in a Rolls Royce and Sunday after Sunday plant that seed thinking that they have not given enough to please or bribe God to reward them. Many of these people live paycheck to paycheck and will neglect their needs so they might have their wants. What surprises me the most is that few, if any, of their fellow congregants are financially blessed, and those few are constantly trotted out before the congregation to give a testimony of how they planted a seed when they were broke and God blessed them. Please remember that in the long con there are people working in concert to dup the conned folks out of their cash, and that is what happens in the church that promotes the prosperity gospel today. If the prosperity gospel worked and people gave all they could afford, then why are so many people across this land out of work? Why are so many people across this land in foreclosure? Why are so many families forced to take their children out of college because the parents can no longer afford the tuition? The answer is simple!

The prosperity gospel is a con, a hoax, a scam used by greedy and nefarious preachers whose only interest is to enrich themselves. And God will judge those prosperity gospel preachers on Judgment Day. I also believe God will judge those folks who adhere to the tenets of the prosperity gospel because it is a false gospel! The U. S. Census indicates that in 2011, the official poverty rate was 15.0 percent. There were 46.2 million people in poverty.

The previously mentioned article on the Prosperity Gospel by Ms. Falani informed us that a large percentage of the middle class are willing participants in the prosperity gospel's doctrine. Hmm, the middle class! Why would someone in the middle class waste their time and money in the pursuit of more materialism when there are so many poor people God would want to bless FIRST? I can understand a poor person falling prey to the prosperity gospel, but any person from the upper and middle class thinking they can bribe God must be greedy, materialistic and an extremely poor steward of what God has given them! I believe that I read somewhere, "to whom much is given, much is required!"

Woe onto both the greedy prosperity preachers and their greedy middle and upper class converts as they should learn to be content with what they have. When I go to heaven, I will not spend one minute looking for them (prosperity gospel preachers and adherents) as I know God is displeased with them! Yes, I am being judgmental!

The Word of God is clear! I love what Paul clearly identifies as the Gospel approved of by God in Galatians 1:6-9, "I am astonished that you are so quickly deserting the one who called you to live in the grace of Christ **and are turning to a different gospel—**⁷**which is really no gospel at all.** Evidently some people are throwing you into confusion and are trying to pervert the gospel of Christ. ⁸But even if we or an angel from heaven should preach a gospel other than the one we preached to you, let them be under God's curse! ⁹As we have already said, so now I say again: If anybody is preaching to you a gospel other than what you accepted, let them be under God's curse!"

My sisters and brothers, there is only one true gospel and that is the Gospel of Jesus Christ! The gospel of Jesus Christ has not, does not and will not teach us to seek wealth over the kingdom of Heaven. Jesus' words on this issue recorded in the Gospel of Mark 8:36 are ever so clear, "What good is it for someone to gain the whole world, yet forfeit their soul?" If I am wrong, **PLEASE SHOW ME THE SCRIPTURE** that supersedes and makes Mark 8:36 null and void and negates Galatians 1:6-9 about the only true gospel.

CHAPTER 7

Tithing versus Giving: Show me the Scripture that Obligates Tithing in the Modern Christian Church

Let me say from the outset that this article is more about cheerful and generous giving than the legalistic and antiquated Biblical teachings regarding tithing. I believe that we should all support our church generously so the needy within our communities will be served. However, I believe that we should not be held to a standard of ten percent as to how much God has blessed us. We need to give generously of our money but also our time by serving in some ministry as opposed to just occupying a space in a "pew" whenever we decide to attend church.

I teach Sunday School, and when the subject of tithing is brought up, I say, "The life, death and resurrection of Jesus Christ removes us from the burden of being under the Law and places us under the banner, the shield of GRACE!" The Apostles Paul, Peter and James all spoke to how difficult it was for the people of Israel to strictly adhere to all the laws and their tenets.

According to the Baker Theological Dictionary of the Bible, "The Laws (traditionally 613 in number) are concentrated in certain passages of the Pentateuch." Interestingly, there were seven laws that preceded the 613 Mosaic laws and they are referred to as the Seven Laws of Noah or the Noahide Laws. An article in Wikipedia.

com entitled **The Seven Laws of Noah** states, "In Judaism, the Seven Laws of Noah, or the Noahide Laws, are a set of moral imperatives that, according to the Talmud, were given by God as a binding set of laws for the "children of Noah"—that is, all of humankind. According to Judaism, any non-Jew who adheres to these laws is regarded as a *righteous gentile*, and is assured of a place in the World to Come, the final reward of the righteous. Adherents are often called "B'nei Noach" (Children of Noah) or "Noahides," and may sometimes network in Jewish synagogues.

The seven laws listed by the Tosefta [a compilation of the Jewish **oral law**] and the Talmud are:

1. The prohibition of Idolatry.
2. The prohibition of Murder.
3. The prohibition of Theft.
4. The prohibition of Sexual immorality.
5. The prohibition of Blasphemy.
6. The prohibition of eating flesh taken from an animal while it is still alive.
7. The requirement of maintaining courts to provide legal recourse.

The Noahide laws comprise the six commandments which were given to Adam in the Garden of Eden, according to the Talmud's interpretation of Gen 2:16, and a seventh precept, which was added after the Flood of Noah. According to Judaism, the 613 commandments given in the **written** Torah, as well as their explanations and applications discussed in the oral Torah, are applicable to the Jews only, **and non-Jews are bound only to observe the seven Noahide laws.**"

With that being said, I have come to understand that there were 613 ancient Jewish Laws spelled out in the Bible and that Jesus and the writers of the New Testament spoke about the difficulty of (1) strict adherence to the Law and (2) that the Law should NOT be a stumbling block to salvation of the non-Jewish Christian converts better known as Gentile believers. The 613 laws were to have a specific life application to the Jews, and all the other nations were bound by the Noahide Laws. Modern day Christians then are not held accountable to or obligated to the Mosaic law of tithing.

Strict adherence to the Law cannot and will not save us; only believing in Jesus can and will! Jewish religious history, law, and tradition, are taught through the **Torah** (the first five books of the Old Testament) and the **Talmud** (which is the Jewish religious book second only in importance to the Torah.) The Talmud is a Rabbinical teaching tool of the Oral and Written Jewish History and law. We must understand then that according to the Torah and the Talmud the Mosaic Laws were strictly applicable for God's Chosen people and no one else. Again, Gentiles were to adhere to the Noahide, or pre-Mosaic laws. To reinforce my point, let us briefly look at scripture. God's Word is specific, and in Leviticus God, Jehovah, Yahweh mentions who His laws are for in the Old Testament era. The NIV translation of Leviticus 28:30-34 states, "[30]A tithe of everything from the land, whether grain from the soil or fruit from the trees, belongs to the LORD; it is holy to the LORD. [31]Whoever would redeem any of their tithe must add a fifth of the value to it. [32]Every tithe of the herd and flock—every tenth animal that passes under the shepherd's rod—will be holy to the LORD. [33]No one may pick out the good from the bad or make any substitution. If anyone does make a substitution, both the animal and its substitute become holy and cannot be redeemed. [34]These are the commands the Lord gave Moses at Mount Sinai for **the Israelites**."

Paying close attention to Leviticus 27:34, we see specifically who God assigned as His messenger to the Israelites regarding the law of tithing, Moses. What specific people His messenger Moses gave the law of tithing to, again, the young nation of Israel, and where the message concerning the law of tithing was delivered, Mt. Sinai. There is absolutely **NO MENTION** of any of the other descendants of Noah mentioned in the Table of Nations located in Genesis, Chapter 10! It is important for us to understand that the Word of God is both balanced and specific! If we were to look at Deuteronomy 4:44-46, we would see the same degree of specificity. "⁴⁴This is the law **Moses** set before the **Israelites**. ⁴⁵These are the stipulations, decrees and laws Moses gave them when they came out of Egypt ⁴⁶**and were in the valley near Beth Peor east of the Jordan, in the land of Sihon king of the Amorites**, who reigned in Heshbon and was defeated by Moses and the Israelites as they came out of Egypt." This pattern of Moses giving God's law to the Israelites at a specific location is a consistent theme throughout the first five books of the Old Testament. No other nations are mentioned as being recipients of God's Law!

So again, my intent here is to encourage folks to cheerfully, regularly and generously give to their House of God in proportion to how God has blessed them and not limit themselves to a law that was not meant for them. And before anyone runs to the church that I attend, New Hope Missionary Baptist Church in Southfield, Michigan to see if I am in fact a cheerful and generous giver, know this: I am retired, so my income has changed, and with the current state of the economy, I support other churches in addition to the one where I am a member. I now spread my offerings among a total of FIVE churches. Three of these churches are within the metropolitan Detroit area and two of them in my hometown of Louisville, Kentucky. There is no Biblical mandate that I am obligated to give all my offerings to the church where I fellowship. I give where I see a need, where the pastor has shown himself approved and is truly teaching God's Word and where I see the ills of the community being addressed. Some of the churches I contribute to are barely making their mortgage payments. Some of their pastors are not accepting a salary just to keep their House of God financially afloat. My conscience, as it relates to Christian giving, is clear!

Paul said that as Christians we should give cheerfully. Hence the adage, "The Lord loves a cheerful giver!" On its website, the Brooke Hill Free Methodist Church posts an article entitled "Giving" on the issue of why we should give to our church, and it states in part, "Biblically" we are commanded to give **cheerfully** (2 Corinthians 9:7 [Each of you should give what you have decided in your heart to give, not reluctantly or under compulsion, for God loves a cheerful giver. NIV]), **generously** (Romans 12:8 {if it is to encourage, then give encouragement; if it is giving, then give generously; if it is to lead, do it diligently; if it is to show mercy, do it cheerfully.}), and **in proportion to what we have been given** (Mark 12:41-44 [41Jesus sat down opposite the place where the offerings were put and watched the crowd putting their money into the temple treasury. Many rich people threw in large amounts. 42But a poor widow came and put in two very small copper coins, worth only a few cents. 43Calling his disciples to him, Jesus said, "Truly I tell you, this poor widow has put more into the treasury than all the others. 44They all gave out of their wealth; but she, out of her poverty, put in everything—all she had to live on."]). After all, when you think about the fact that all that you have has been given to you by the Lord, giving a portion of it back just makes sense—it's not yours in the first place!"

Here is an illustration of what I perceive to be a cheerful giver. Recently, two families split a Powerball jackpot that was over a half billion dollars. I believe after taxes these families each walked away with over 200 million dollars. For the sake of my argument, let us say they each received 250 million dollars. Okay, what would their tithes be? If my math serves me correctly their tithes would be 25 million dollars, ten percent. But what if they gave 50 million dollars to their church and Christian based community organizations that feed and address the needs of the poor? Would they still be rich? What if they gave half of their winnings (125 million dollars) to their church? Would they still be rich? The answer would be an unequivocal and resounding YES! But if they were to only tithe, are they being REAL with GOD who has blessed them beyond their wildest imaginations?

My point is that if you can afford to give more than the perceived "I am good because I gave ten percent," then do that. If you can afford to give 20 to 50 percent and are still blessed, do that. But, whatever you give, make sure you give because of your love for God and His Son Jesus, not because you want to impress your fellow congregants and pastor.

If you noticed, I used the word "afford" twice above. This word, "afford" is one of the most over-used and exploited words in all the English language when it comes to giving. People will use the excuse that they cannot AFFORD to give more to God because of their massive bills. But how do we get or accumulate extremely high bills??? **The envelope please!** If we cannot give to God in proportion to how He is blessing us, then we are NOT living within the confines of our blessings or our means! Who says we should live a champagne lifestyle when God has blessed us to live on a Kool Aid budget? Let us take a moment and delve into this elusive word, "afford". Webster's defines afford thusly: "to manage to bear without serious detriment." Without serious detriment! What I know is happening in this society are two things. First, most Americans have a false sense of entitlement. We feel that since we live in the wealthiest and most technologically advanced country in the world, we should have all the desires of our hearts. And I repeat, some folks feel they should have ALL THE DESIRES of their Heart! Second, since we feel entitled, we are conspirators to the theory of conspicuous consumption. I have a young nephew, and we have had many conversations about his spending habits, especially as it relates to the incredible amount of money he spends on the latest Nike basketball shoes. I have known of his spending upwards of $150 just so he can have the latest Jordan's or Lebron James shoes that he knows he will only wear a few times before the next, "Must Have a Pair" basketball shoes are introduced to the marketplace. I encourage him constantly to forget about the shoes and save his money for the future, but he and his peers are aided and abetted by their parents in this economically devastating game of conspicuous consumption. I imagine that these same parents do not give $150 a month or even quarterly to their church on their children's behalf but have $150 for a damn pair; yes I said DAMN pair of basketball shoes! I have money for some stupid shoes but no money for the Lord!

So, when I hear folks say they do not have any money left over to put something in the offering plate, I truly understand because they have other priorities for their money and have a "I will pay God with whatever I have left over after I buy my fine clothes, car and shoes!" Tithing, or giving for them, is a neglected financial option, one they have been aware of all their Christian days.

At a church quarterly business meeting I learned that about 20 percent of the congregation tithes. Tithing to that 20 percent then is a means to comply with an outdated Biblical concept that only applied to God's Chosen People! Show me the scriptures where as a religious mandate the Egyptians, Chaldeans, Babylonians, Greeks, or Romans or any other Old or New Testament non-Jewish nation were obligated to tithe. The ancient non-Jewish people of the Old and New Testament era were called Gentiles. Where was the New Testament legal mandate for the Gentiles to tithe? No, tithing was an Old Testament legal requirement for the ancient Israelites and does not apply today to the Modern Christian. If tithing were a Christian mandate, then why did not Jesus talk about and teach about it? Where is the parable on tithing as parables were the most common way that Jesus taught religious and life application lessons to the people of His day?

One only needs to check a Strong's Exhaustive Concordance and he would discover that on the three occasions Jesus spoke of tithing, He was admonishing the Pharisees for their being hypocritical tithers so they might brag about being legalistically and righteously obedient to God's Law. The Pharisees believed that total obedience to God's law would get them into heaven. But they were not aware that God looked at whether or not their motives were pure. God knew what was in their hearts and judged them accordingly!

The New Testament authors never spoke of tithing as a Christian obligation; rather, they spoke, as Paul did, about giving generously, cheerfully, and regularly, especially to support the poor! And let me say that the tithes were not to be used to pay pastor's salaries as they are today. In the New Testament era the congregation gave money to their pastors (I Corinthians 9:7-14; Philippians 4:10-19), and many preachers like the Apostle Paul made their own living so as not to be a financial burden on their church (Acts 18:3). The tithes were not to be used for the building fund as in the New Testament era the Jews paid a temple tax or drachma or didrachma, a Greek coin paid to the Levites to support the operation of the temple. An example of the requirement of this temple tax was mentioned when Jesus instructed Peter to take the money out of the mouth of a fish before they entered the synagogue to worship (Matthew 17:24-27).

But Brother James, did you not say your father was a Baptist preacher? Did he teach tithing in his church? And if he did, why are you promoting this heretical doctrine of not tithing? Great question! And yes, my father did preach and teach about tithing as he did not have all the hermeneutical study tools and Biblical knowledge we have available to us today. Yes, my father, like many well-meaning pastors today, did not make the connection that two major events eradicated the legal tenets of tithing for the Christians. First, the role of the Levites who were entrusted with maintaining the tithes for the maintenance of the temple/Tabernacle was ended in the Old Testament era and was null and void during the Christian era. According to the Wycliffe Bible Dictionary, "With the destruction of the Jewish state and the temple in A. D. 70, the Old Testament Hebrew priesthood [the Levites] vanished from history. Attempts were made for a while subsequent to that date to continue some parts of the priestly and sacrificial system, but these proved unsuccessful and they soon ceased completely." Second, when Jesus came He ushered in a New Priesthood. Again, referring to the Wycliffe Bible Dictionary, "The Hebrew priesthood, then, though it is for the most part fulfilled in Christ in the New Testament, in a limited sense is also fulfilled in the New Testament Church. The ephemeral priesthood of Aaron and his sons fades into **uselessness** when Christ comes as the perfect intermediary and intercessor as well as the perfect sacrifice for His people and their sins."

Logic dictates that if God established the Levites as an Israelite tribe set aside to do his work, part of which was handling the tithes, and their role disappeared in the New Testament era, would not the collection of tithes also be eliminated? Would not God want us to be cheerful givers not feeling legally obligated as we are today in paying local, state and federal taxes? Would not God want us to give, and more importantly, give in proportion to how He has blessed us? Would not Jesus be the greatest proponent of tithing in the New Testament if God wanted the Christian Church to continue tithing? Why is there no similar statement of "bring me all the tithes into the storehouse" in the New Testament? Again, after the fall of Jerusalem in 70 A.D., the Levitical roles and responsibilities were eliminated. The only mention of the word, "storehouse" in the New Testament is found in Luke 12:24, where the Revised Standard Version (RSV) translation reads, "Consider the ravens: they neither sow nor reap, they have neither **storehouse** nor barn, and yet God feeds them. Of how much more value are you than the birds!" This does not remotely sound like a message to Christians to tithe!

I respectfully suggest that the eradication of tithing was and is a test God has placed upon His people, you and me! I believe He is saying if you truly love me, then you will give regularly, sometimes sacrificially, cheerfully and generously without compulsion, to support the good works associated with the teachings of my Son, Jesus Christ! I remember when the church I attend was building a new sanctuary...the financial sacrifices some of us made to ensure we moved into a new and beautiful edifice. Some people gave well beyond their means, like the little old lady Jesus mentioned to His Disciples as an example of giving (Mark 12:41-44).

You cannot show me any scriptures that indicate that tithing is a New Testament obligation, and we certainly live in the New Testament or should I really say the Christian era! I am not a heretic, just one who attempts to study the word of God and wants to be crystal clear on God's Word. No, I am not a heretic but a practitioner of the Biblical study principles and process of hermeneutics. Hermeneutics is the art and science of proper Biblical interpretation by focusing on the grammatical, contextual and historical content of the scriptures, hence my stance on tithing.

The New Testament writers all spoke to the issue of rejecting the Mosaic Law as a requirement for salvation and eternal life (Galatians 3:13-14; Hebrews 8:13). Jesus even warned the people of His day to beware of the teachers of the Law (Mark 12:38-39). Certainly I would never postulate that the Book of Acts should be viewed and revered as the basis of Christian doctrine, but there was a major issue that had to be resolved by the Council of Jerusalem in Acts, Chapter 15.

To see what this problem was, let us look at Acts 15: 5, "Then some of the believers who belonged to the party of the Pharisees stood up and said, "**The Gentiles must be circumcised and required to keep the Law of Moses.**""

Keep the Law of Moses! Wow! The Hebraic Christians found it difficult to keep the 613 Mosaic laws, and now they wanted to harness the gentile converts to Christianity with this curse. Let us look a little further in Acts 15. Acts 15:6-11, "⁶The apostles and elders met to consider this question. ⁷After much discussion, Peter got up and addressed them: 'Brothers, you know that some time ago God made a choice among you that the Gentiles might hear from my lips the message of the gospel and believe. ⁸God, who knows the heart, showed that he accepted them by giving the **Holy Spirit** to them, just as he did to us. ⁹He did not discriminate between us and them, for he purified their hearts by faith. ¹⁰Now then, why do you try to test God by putting on the necks of Gentiles a yoke that neither we nor our ancestors have been able to bear? ¹¹No! We believe it is through the grace of our Lord Jesus that we are saved, just as they are.'"

The discussion of the apostle, elders and disciples on this important doctrinal issue came to be known as the Council of Jerusalem. We need to look at Acts 15:22-29, where we will see what was decided and communicated via a letter to the gentile Christian converts; "²²Then the apostles and elders, with the whole church, decided to choose some of their own men and send them to Antioch with Paul and Barnabas. They chose Judas (called Barsabbas) and Silas, men who were leaders among the believers. ²³With them they sent the following letter:

> The apostles and elders, your brothers,
>
> To the Gentile believers in Antioch, Syria and Cilicia:
>
> Greetings.
>
> ²⁴We have heard that some went out from us **without our authorization** and disturbed you, troubling your minds by what they said. ²⁵So we all agreed to choose some men and send them to you with our dear friends Barnabas and Paul— ²⁶men who have risked their lives for the name of our Lord Jesus Christ. ²⁷Therefore we are sending Judas and Silas to confirm by word of mouth what we are writing. ²⁸It seemed good to the **Holy Spirit and to us** not to burden you with anything beyond the following requirements: ²⁹You are to abstain from food sacrificed to idols, from blood, from the meat of strangled animals and from sexual immorality. You will do well to avoid these things.
>
> Farewell.

Now again, I do not subscribe to the theory postulated by some Christian denominations that Acts contains Christian practicable doctrine, but we must consider that at the Council of Jerusalem the **Holy Spirit** was present to help in the decision making process of the Church leaders. This undeniable fact, the presence of the Holy Spirit is attested to in Acts 15:28 , "It seemed good to the **Holy Spirit** and to us not to burden you with anything beyond the following requirements:" There is no mention of circumcision, and more importantly tithing being a requirement for a non-Jewish person, a gentile to become a Christian.

What I am implying is that if tithing was still a valid and practicable law, a Godly obligation, why then was it not mentioned in the three requirements for new Christian converts mentioned in Acts 15:29? Please do not get me wrong at this juncture. I still hold steadfast to my position that we must give and give cheerfully, regularly and generously to assist the good works God desires within our respective communities and churches.

Okay, I know you are growing weary of me, but just hear me out for a while longer so I might make my point. Please allow me to use the words of the Apostle Paul in his epistle/letter to the church in Galatia regarding the negation of the Mosaic Law which would include tithing after the life, ministry, death and resurrection of Jesus Christ. In Galatians 2:15-16 Paul wrote, [15]"We who are Jews by birth and not sinful Gentiles [16]**know that a person is not justified by the works of the law, but by faith in Jesus Christ.** So we, too, have put our faith in Christ Jesus that we may be justified by faith in Christ and **not by the works of the law**, because by the works of the law no one will be justified."

So what is Paul saying? He is saying that only our faith in Jesus is important, not adherence to the law. Oh, by the way, when was the last time you ate some bacon and or ham? They are forbidden by the law!

Let us look at another scripture in Galatians to help me validate my point on giving versus tithing. Galatians 3:23-25 (NIV) states, "[23]Before the coming of this faith, we were held in custody under the law, locked up until the faith that was to come would be revealed. [24]So the law was our guardian until Christ came that we might be justified by faith. [25]Now that this faith has come, we are no longer under a guardian [the law]."

Paul was speaking directly to the Jewish converts to Christianity, and if the law was only for the chosen people, and now Paul is saying it is null and void, how then is the law of tithing applicable to the Christian congregations of today?

I am more in favor of giving offerings as opposed to tithing as the apostles said in proportion to how God has blessed us than strictly adhering to an antiquated Old Testament mandate that again, only spoke to God's Chosen people!

So, if tithing was a Biblical mandate only for the Chosen People (the Jews), then why do so many modern churches preach and teach tithing? I have two possible answers. First, there are some pastors that realize that without tithing and a Biblical command for that LAW their congregants would feel free to only remit what they have left over after they have rewarded their hard work with whatever luxuries they can and cannot afford. People have a tendency to look at God as a friend, a paternalistic, or should I say, philanthropic father figure who will not mind if I spend large sums of money at the club or on the desires of my heart without thinking that God's house has bills just as my house has bills. After all, who has been to heaven and returned telling us about a wonderful life "up there"! Maybe I need to enjoy life here on earth just in case there is no heaven as Bill Maher so frequently suggests! These are misguided notions that I certainly do not practice.

God, who is the creator of all things, does not need us for anything; however, we need God, and given His mandate that we come together and fellowship, then we need to understand that we must financially support our respective house of worship. God could but does not just zap a sanctuary onto a specific land site and then say, "enter and praise me and all will be taken care of." NO, God expects us to honor Him by putting aside some of the money He has blessed us with in direct proportion to how He has blessed us financially. He also expects us to set aside time to work in His vineyard to glorify and praise His name. We would rather give money than time any day and that is a fallacy we must overcome!

What I am hopefully saying with fervor and without sounding like a blasphemer is that we should have a philanthropic mindset when it comes to giving. We should, as the Apostle Paul said, give in direct proportion to how God is blessing us. Tithing then is legalistic, meaning I can give ten percent when I could afford to give fifteen percent and feel that I have done the right thing.

Many years ago I read in the Daily Word, "God blesses us to bless others!" That concept stuck with me and is my giving mantras for those less fortunate than I. Even when we consider the purpose of tithes, they were to be used to

1. praise and honor God,
2. feed the poor and hungry,
3. address the needs of the widows and orphans within the Jewish community, and
4. take care of the needs of foreigners (the Bible refers to them as aliens) travelling and distressed in Jewish territories. But today, we pay tithes to build elaborate sanctuaries and to pay our pastor an exorbitant salary so he or she might live the lifestyle of the rich and famous.

There is one more historical point I would like to share with you before I close that will hopefully reinforce all that I have said. The very controversial Bible teacher, the late L. Ray Smith, in an internet article entitled, "Tithing is Unscriptural Under the New Covenant: A Scriptural Exposition on the Fraudulent Fleecing of the Flock," wrote, "**We** have

Scriptural proof that no such law or custom as Christian tithing was taught or practiced in the Church by the early apostles." Their epistles are totally devoid of any such tithing custom or law. Gentile converts were never taught to tithe to anyone. Although the temple and priesthood in Jerusalem remained until 70 **AD**, not even Jewish converts were taught to give their tithes to the Apostles rather than to the temple priests.

In the Acts 15 Jerusalem Conference we find outlined what the apostles all agreed was necessary for the newly converted Gentiles to practice, and by inspiration of the Holy Spirit of God, tithing is conspicuously missing. Some believing Pharisees *wanted* the apostles to teach the Gentiles to keep the Law of Moses (which certainly contained the law of tithing, Acts 15:5), but the apostles headed by Peter, James, and Paul would not hear of it (Acts 15:28-29)! Yet, what is one of the very first legislated duties taught to Gentile converts by the Church today? It is that they must tithe their annual salaries to the Church. Where did this unscriptural law of Christian tithing come from?

Notice this telling bit of history from the *Britannica*, "**Tithes in Christendom**—The earliest authentic example of anything like a law of the State enforcing payment appears to occur in the capitularies [ecclesiasticals] of Charlemagne at the end of the 8th or beginning of the 9th century. Tithes were by that enactment to be applied to the maintenance of the bishop, clergy, the poor, and the fabric of the church. In the course of time the principle of payment of tithes was extended FAR BEYOND its original intention. Thus they became transferable to laymen and saleable like ordinary property, in spite of the injunctions of the third Lateran Council; and they became payable OUT OF SOURCES OF INCOME [not just farming and herding, but other trades and occupations and salaries paid in the form of money] NOT ORIGINALLY TITHABLE." (1963, volume 22, page 253, 'TITHES')." Smith, goes even further on the issue that modern Christians are not

Biblically mandated to tithe and states, "The Catholic Church knows its own history. Here is how tithing got back into the Church after being absent for nearly five centuries: "As the Church expanded and various institutions arose, it became necessary to make laws which would insure the proper and permanent support of the clergy. The payment of tithes was adopted from the Old Law... The earliest positive legislation on the subject seems to be contained in the letter of the bishops assembled at Tours in 567 and the [canons] of the Council of Macon in 585."—*The Catholic Encyclopedia.*'"

Smith may have been controversial and I certainly do not subscribe to his views on the Trinity and the non-existence of hell. But on the issue of tithing he makes a good argument which is supported by historical facts and sources!

So, please, after reading this discourse, learn to give beyond 10 percent if you can afford it. I believe that if you are a faithful Christian who has through no fault of your own fallen on hard times, God will understand if your offerings are less than ten percent. Remember the widow who gave the two pennies? Stop paying yourself first before paying God with your leftovers. Stop thinking that because God is God he does not need your financial contributions. Start giving God what you know He is deserving of in the form of money and time (working in a ministry)! God loves a cheerful giver, so give as much as you realistically can being a good steward of your God given blessings.

I know I am correct on the issue of tithing versus giving, but if you believe me to be wrong and continue to hold on to an antiquated biblical tenet, then show me the scripture. I could be wrong, but I do not think so!

Epilogue

In the Final Analysis

[11]and to make it your ambition to lead a quiet life: You should mind your own business and work with your hands, just as we told you, [12]so that your daily life may win the respect of outsiders and so that you will not be dependent on anybody. (1 Thessalonians 4:11-12 NIV)

Well, I warned you from the outset. I warned you that I am very opinionated, but my opinions are based upon what I have read and what I have studied under those religious leaders that I sincerely respect. I truly respect those pastors who use a hermeneutical approach to both their studies and teachings. Too many preachers teach from a vantage point that will make them appear to their naïve congregations to be gods on earth while in my mind those pastors are merely demigods, ans some of them use and abuse the True Word of God only to enrich themselves and their families. The scripture is replete with warnings to Christians about the false prophets, false preachers and teachers.

Please understand one undeniable truth that is applicable to each chapter I have presented to you. That fact is that your pastor is not the final arbitrator of God's word. God's word is the final arbitrator of God's word. Too often after a church service I will hear people say, "my pastor said," and I immediately ponder what does the word of God say in context to what their pastor said during the course of his/her sermon. Again, I am not hating on any pastor because I know there are some that are truly dedicated to preaching and teaching God's word. But then there are those others who are not!

I sincerely pray that if I have offended you in any way through my writings, that you will do your research and show me the scriptures that justify the garbage emanating from many pulpits across this land related to the aforementioned subjects.

The scripture commands me, even though we may not know one another or ever meet in this life, to love you as I love myself. I have committed myself to do that, and if I am wrong, then you need to show me the scripture where I am not supposed to love you!

Thanks for hearing me out!

Brother James.

www.ingramcontent.com/pod-product-compliance
Lightning Source LLC
Chambersburg PA
CBHW070654050426
42451CB00008B/341